Philippians

The Treasures of Joy

Philippians

The Treasures of Joy

Dr. Bo Wagner

Word of His Mouth Publishers
Mooresboro, NC

All Scripture quotations are taken from the **King James Version** of the Bible.

ISBN: 978-1-941039-42-7
Printed in the United States of America
©2024 Dr. Bo Wagner

Word of His Mouth Publishers
Mooresboro, NC
www.wordofhismouth.com

Table of Contents

Introduction

There is usually a reason why people write a letter. And with Paul, it would be more accurate to say that there was always a reason why he wrote a letter. In Galatians, we find that a **problem** precipitated him writing that letter; people had slipped in and convinced the Galatian believers to lay aside the liberty they had in Christ and to once again go back to being enslaved in a yoke of bondage. In Ephesians, we find that a **doctrine** precipitated him writing that letter; he wanted them to know that Christ had predestined Gentile believers to be in the household of faith on an equal plane with believing Jews.

But when we get to Philippians, we find the most unique thing for a man like Paul. It was not at all odd for him to write about problems or doctrines; he did a great deal of that. But the Epistle to the Philippians was not precipitated by a problem or a doctrine; it was precipitated by an **emotion**! And it only took him four verses to get around to mentioning that emotion:

Philippians 1:4 *Always in every prayer of mine for you all making request with joy,*

In this short book of just four chapters, he will use the word joy six times. For a bit of perspective on that, Philippians is one of Paul's shortest letters, and yet, he mentions joy more times in Philippians than in any other letter he wrote! Both Romans and 1 Corinthians are four times as long as Philippians, yet neither of them has as many mentions of joy as Philippians does. He also uses the words "rejoice" eight times, "rejoiced" one time, and "rejoicing" one time.

And this ought to really catch our attention. Yes, Paul will deal with a problem or two in this book, and he will certainly teach doctrine in this book, but he wrote this book as a personal letter to people that he was just joyful over.

And that is why I call Philippians *The Treasures Of Joy.*

Chapter One
I Have You in My Heart

Philippians 1:1 P*aul and Timotheus, the servants of Jesus Christ, to all the saints in Christ Jesus which are at Philippi, with the bishops and deacons:* **2** *Grace be unto you, and peace, from God our Father, and from the Lord Jesus Christ.* **3** *I thank my God upon every remembrance of you,* **4** *Always in every prayer of mine for you all making request with joy,* **5** *For your fellowship in the gospel from the first day until now;* **6** *Being confident of this very thing, that he which hath begun a good work in you will perform it until the day of Jesus Christ:* **7** *Even as it is meet for me to think this of you all, because I have you in my heart; inasmuch as both in my bonds, and in the defence and confirmation of the gospel, ye all are partakers of my grace.* **8** *For God is my record, how greatly I long after you all in the bowels of Jesus Christ.*

The greeting

Philippians 1:1 *Paul and Timotheus, the servants of Jesus Christ, to all the saints in Christ Jesus which are at Philippi, with the bishops and deacons:* **2** *Grace be unto you, and peace, from God our Father, and from the Lord Jesus Christ.*

As Paul was writing these words, it was about A.D. 61 or 62, some ten years after he first set foot in Philippi. He was right then in his first imprisonment in Rome and not sure how things were going to come out for him. But we really need to begin this study by going back to where Paul first got to know the Philippians; it is very significant to all that he says within the book.

Acts 16:8 *And they passing by Mysia came down to Troas.* **9** *And a vision appeared to Paul in the night; There stood a man of Macedonia, and prayed him, saying, Come over into Macedonia, and help us.* **10** *And after he had seen the vision, immediately we endeavoured to go into Macedonia, assuredly gathering that the Lord had called us for to preach the gospel unto them.* **11** *Therefore loosing from Troas, we came with a straight course to Samothracia, and the next day to Neapolis;* **12** *And from thence to Philippi, which is the chief city of that part of Macedonia, and a colony: and we were in that city abiding certain days.*

This is a record from Paul's second missionary journey, and it is where Paul first got to Philippi. But it is not just where Paul first got to Philippi; it is where the gospel first got to Philippi. And this is incredibly significant because of where Philippi was. Philippi, the chief city of Macedonia, was in southeastern Europe. This is where the gospel message first got to Europe, which should mean everything to us because it got to us from Europe! We are sitting here saved today because Paul answered the Macedonian call and traveled to Philippi.

While he was there, he won the first converts to Christ in that area:

Acts 16:13 *And on the sabbath we went out of the city by a river side, where prayer was wont to be made; and we sat down, and spake unto the women which resorted thither.* **14** *And a certain woman named Lydia, a seller of purple, of the city of Thyatira, which worshipped God, heard us: whose heart the Lord opened, that she attended unto the things which were spoken of Paul.* **15** *And when she was baptized, and her* household, she besought us, saying, If ye have judged me to be faithful to the Lord, come into my house, and abide there. And she constrained us.

He also ran into proof that the devil made it there before the gospel did:

Acts 16:16 *And it came to pass, as we went to prayer, a certain damsel possessed with a spirit of divination met us, which brought her masters much gain by soothsaying:* **17** *The same followed Paul and us, and cried, saying, These men are the servants of the most high God, which shew unto us the way of salvation.* **18** *And this did she many days. But Paul, being grieved, turned and said to the spirit, I command thee in the name of Jesus Christ to come out of her. And he came out the same hour.*

This did not go over so well with people who had a financial stake in this girl's problem:

Acts 16:19 *And when her masters saw that the hope of their gains was gone, they caught Paul and Silas, and drew them into the marketplace unto the rulers,* **20** *And brought them to the magistrates, saying, These men, being Jews, do exceedingly trouble our city,* **21** *And teach customs, which are not lawful for us to receive, neither to observe, being Romans.* **22** *And the multitude rose up together against them: and the magistrates rent off their clothes, and commanded to beat them.*

Paul and Silas were now about to be the first people to suffer for Christ in Europe:

Acts 16:23 *And when they had laid many stripes upon them, they cast them into prison, charging the jailor to keep them safely:* **24** *Who, having received such a charge, thrust them into the inner prison, and made their feet fast in the stocks.*

Most everyone knows what happened from there. Paul and Silas sang and praised God at midnight; God shook the prison and opened all of the doors; the jailer thought everyone had escaped and was about to kill himself, and Paul stopped him.

The jailer then got saved, everyone in his family got saved, and he tended to their wounds.

The next day, the magistrates sent some underlings to just "let them go." But then Paul did something no one expected: he pulled the Roman card and actually got a quite understandable "attitude" with them:

Acts 16:37 *But Paul said unto them, They have beaten us openly uncondemned, being Romans, and have cast us into prison; and now do they thrust us out privily? nay verily; but let them come themselves and fetch us out.* **38** *And the serjeants told these words unto the magistrates: and they feared, when they heard that they were Romans.*

In case you are not aware of what all of that was about, please let me fill in the gaps for you. Being a Roman citizen came with certain privileges. One of those privileges was that no one could imprison or abuse you unless you had been tried and found guilty in a proper trial in a court of law. And the harshest punishment for violating this was severe, severe as in being put to death and having all of your possessions taken away. So these magistrates were very literally scared to death!

Acts 16:38 *And the serjeants told these words unto the magistrates: and they feared, when they heard that they were Romans.* **39** *And they came and besought them, and brought them out, and desired them to depart out of the city.* **40** *And they went out of the prison, and entered into the house of Lydia: and when they had seen the brethren, they comforted them, and departed.*

Here is how Paul described all of that some years later:

1 Thessalonians 2:2 *But even after that we had suffered before, and were shamefully entreated, as ye know, at Philippi, we were bold in our God to speak unto you the gospel of God with much contention.*

So, after all of that, how did the Philippian believers become the people that Paul got such joy from even years later? Here is part of the answer:

Philippians 4:15 *Now ye Philippians know also, that in the beginning of the gospel, when I departed from Macedonia, no church communicated with me as concerning giving and receiving, but ye only.* **16** *For even in Thessalonica ye sent once and again unto my necessity.*

As far as we can tell from the New Testament record, the church at Philippi seems to have been the only one that supported Paul as a missionary! He was giving his entire life to get the gospel to the world, and it never seems to have occurred to anyone else to think, "It really isn't right for Paul to be working day and night for free; we need to support him!"

Look how well they took care of him:

Philippians 4:18 *But I have all, and abound: I am full, having received of Epaphroditus the things which were sent from you, an odour of a sweet smell, a sacrifice acceptable, wellpleasing to God.*

And these people were not rich! Look at how Paul described the churches of Macedonia, which included the Philippians, to the Corinthians:

2 Corinthians 8:1 *Moreover, brethren, we do you to wit of the grace of God bestowed on the churches of Macedonia;* **2** *How that in a great trial of affliction the abundance of their joy and their deep poverty abounded unto the riches of their liberality.*

These people were hearing the gospel for the first time ever; they were Gentiles to the core. They had never been taught, and yet they loved Paul so much that in spite of their poverty, they took incredibly good care of him as he traveled around the world, starting churches. The Philippians are the clearest example in the Bible of what supporting missionaries looks like.

And as we will see when we get to the end of it, this letter that Paul wrote to them is basically a thank you note for that support!

Now that you understand the background, look at the first couple of verses once more.

Philippians 1:1 *Paul and Timotheus, the servants of Jesus Christ, to all the saints in Christ Jesus which are at Philippi, with the bishops and deacons:* **2** *Grace be unto you, and peace, from God our Father, and from the Lord Jesus Christ.*

While Paul was the author of this letter, he mentioned Timothy right here in verse one. You see, Paul had been to Philippi twice, once as we saw in Acts 16 and then once again later in Acts 20, and Timothy had been with him both times. And, as Paul was writing the letter, Timothy was right there with him in Rome:

Philippians 2:19 *But I trust in the Lord Jesus to send Timotheus shortly unto you, that I also may be of good comfort, when I know your state.*

So the people in Philippi knew Timothy and had a great deal of respect for him, and thus, Paul mentioned him early on in the letter.

Notice that in verse one, Paul referred to both himself and Timothy as the "servants of Jesus Christ." In a great many instances, Paul made a point of calling himself an apostle. But he did not do so here for one very obvious reason: the Philippians never questioned that. To them, he was not just an apostle; he was their apostle, the one who hazarded his life to keep them from going to hell.

He addressed the believers in Philippi as "the saints in Christ Jesus." These Gentiles loved their Jewish apostle, and Paul respected his Gentile converts! But he also did one other pretty unusual thing in verse one:

Philippians 1:1 *Paul and Timotheus, the servants of Jesus Christ, to all the saints in Christ Jesus which are at Philippi, with the bishops and deacons:*

Notice that mention of bishops and deacons; it is significant. Here is what Jamieson, Fausset, and Brown said of this:

"This is the earliest letter of Paul where bishops and deacons are mentioned, and the only one where they are separately addressed in the salutation. This accords with the probable course of events, deduced alike from the letters and history. While the apostles were constantly visiting the churches in person or by messengers, regular pastors would be less needed; but when some were removed by various causes, provision for the permanent order of the churches would be needed. Hence the three pastoral letters, subsequent to this Epistle, give instruction as to the due appointment of bishops and deacons. It agrees with this new want of the Church, when other apostles were dead or far away, and Paul long in prison, that bishops and deacons should be prominent for the first time in the opening salutation. The Spirit thus intimated that the churches were to look up to their own pastors, now that the miraculous gifts were passing into God's ordinary providence, and the presence of the inspired apostles, the dispensers of those gifts, was to be withdrawn." (424)

In summary, apostles were a one generation gift that was passing away, and the care of the church was being handed off to pastors and deacons.

Philippians 1:2 *Grace be unto you, and peace, from God our Father, and from the Lord Jesus Christ.*

This was a common greeting from Paul:

Ephesians 1:2 *Grace be to you, and peace, from God our Father, and from the Lord Jesus Christ.*

Romans 1:7 *To all that be in Rome, beloved of God, called to be saints: Grace to you and peace from God our Father, and the Lord Jesus Christ.*

1 Corinthians 1:3 *Grace be unto you, and peace, from God our Father, and from the Lord Jesus Christ.*

2 Corinthians 1:2 *Grace be to you and peace from God our Father, and from the Lord Jesus Christ.*

Galatians 1:3 *Grace be to you and peace from God the Father, and from our Lord Jesus Christ,*

Philippians 1:2 *Grace be unto you, and peace, from God our Father, and from the Lord Jesus Christ.*

Colossians 1:2 *To the saints and faithful brethren in Christ which are at Colosse: Grace be unto you, and peace, from God our Father and the Lord Jesus Christ.*

2 Thessalonians 1:2 *Grace unto you, and peace, from God our Father and the Lord Jesus Christ.*

As to the doctrinal content of this verse, the same thing is true here as when he wrote the same words to the believers in Ephesus. Paul fondly desired that the Philippian believers be granted grace and peace from God the Father and from the Lord Jesus Christ.

He knew, of course, that all the world in general is the recipient of the grace of God:

Titus 2:11 *For the grace of God that bringeth salvation hath appeared to all men,*

He also clearly knew that the Philippians had personally, individually received the saving grace of God:

Philippians 1:1 *Paul and Timotheus, the servants of Jesus Christ, to all the **saints** in Christ Jesus...*

What he was desiring for them, and for us, therefore, in verse two, was the daily grace of God, God continuing to give them all the good things day by day that they did not deserve.

As to the peace that he desired for them, and for us, that was obviously not being brought into peace with God in

16

salvation that he wrote of in Colossians 1:20, since, again, they already had that. Just as with grace, this was a daily peace that he was wishing for them and for us, peace that transcends our circumstances. Here is how he expressed it a bit later in this book:

Philippians 4:7 *And the peace of God, which passeth all understanding, shall keep your hearts and minds through Christ Jesus.*

So, Paul loved these dear people in Philippi; he was writing a letter of joy to them, and he was asking for God to grant them grace and peace.

The gratitude

Philippians 1:3 *I thank my God upon every remembrance of you,*

In the writings of Paul, you often find him being very gracious in his words toward his readers. One of the ways that he very commonly did that was by telling them how grateful he was for them. But there is a difference between what he said to others and what he said to the Philippians. When he wrote to the Philippians, he used the words "every remembrance." He told them, quite simply, that every single time they came to his mind, he stopped and thanked God for them. He did not use those exact words of anyone else.

These Philippian believers had made themselves very dear indeed to Paul.

The glow

Philippians 1:4 *Always in every prayer of mine for you all making request with joy,* **5** *For your fellowship in the gospel from the first day until now;*

In verse three, Paul told the Philippians that he always thanked God for them every single time they came to his mind. In these verses, he begins to tell them why. And he began by using two universal absolutes in his very first phrase. Notice it again:

Always in every prayer of mine for you all making request with joy.

From time to time, people tend to speak in hyperbole. But the way Paul so carefully phrased this let the Philippians know that he meant it very literally. Absolutely positively each and every time he prayed for them, he did so *"making request with joy."* There were no exceptions; this was an all the time, every time thing.

Something that you should know at this point that will help you understand the verse is that both the word prayer and the word request are from the same root word, the word *dehaysis.* So what he is saying is, "Whatever I pray for you, no matter when I pray it, I pray that prayer with joy."

It is almost inconceivable that we could ever have anyone that we pray for and all of those prayers be with joy. And yet that was the exact case with Paul and his beloved Philippian believers. And one of the reasons he was able to do so is found in the continuation of the sentence in the very next verse:

Philippians 1:5 *For your fellowship in the gospel from the first day until now;*

That little preposition "for" that begins verse five means upon, or "on the basis of." Paul was able to make all of his prayer requests for them joyful prayer requests for, on the basis of the fact that they had been in "the fellowship of the gospel" with him from the very first day until the day that he was putting pen to parchment to write that epistle. And the word "in" in that phrase means "unto" or "toward." So this was not a statement of the fact that they had been born again; this was a statement of the fact that since the day they got born again, they had partnered with him in getting the gospel to the rest of the world!

Many people who are truly born again either take a long time to develop this type of heart for the lost world, or in the worst of cases, never do. But that was not the case with the Philippians. From the moment they got saved, their attitude was, "We aren't going to hell anymore; everybody needs to get what we just got! What do you need? What can we do to help make that happen?"

That should legitimately be the heart attitude of every single born-again child of God.

Philippians 1:6 *Being confident of this very thing, that he which hath begun a good work in you will perform it until the day of Jesus Christ:*

Paul has been referencing the Philippians' partnership in the gospel, that saving message of the death, burial, and resurrection of the Lord Jesus Christ. From that look at their desire to see the entire world saved, Paul segues in verse six to their own salvation and how very secure it is. He began by saying, *"Being confident of this very thing..."* Being confident is from the word *pepoithose*, which means "to be completely persuaded," and it is in the perfect tense. And here is why all of that is important. All of that means that Paul was absolutely, utterly forever persuaded and that nothing would happen to ever change it. So, this was not something that Paul was merely "pretty sure about;" it is something that he knew beyond any shadow of a doubt because God had made it clear to him. And what he was so convinced of was that, concerning those who believe in Christ, *"he which hath begun a good work in you will perform it until the day of Jesus Christ."*

The reason why these words must apply to every believer in Christ and not just the Philippians is that since salvation is always by the grace of God and never by our works, every good work of salvation in every heart is always and only begun, originated from God.

Notice the promise once again: *"he which hath begun a good work in you will perform it until the day of Jesus Christ:"*

The word "perform" is significant. It is from the word *epitelesie*. It means "to bring something to perfect completion." In other words, our salvation is not something that has the potential of not being completed!

On the way to South Carolina from our church, not too far from my house, there is a development of really large and lovely homes. But right out in front of that development of really large and lovely homes, there is one home standing as a very stark contrast to all of the rest. It was very clearly intended to be just like all of the others: two-story, brick, garage, expensive. But for some reason that no one has ever been able to tell me that one home out of all the others was never finished. It was about eighty percent finished, by my estimation. And for the last ten years or so, as I have passed by multiple times a week, it has deteriorated further and further and further. It is an eyesore and a testimony to a project that was started but never completed.

No one's salvation will ever, ever, ever be like that! And the reason that no one's salvation will ever be like that is because we did not begin the process of our salvation nor are we responsible for completing the process of our salvation. The very same One who began our salvation is the very One who is in charge of bringing our salvation to perfect completion. God started it; God maintains it; God will finish it. If it were up to us, any of us, our salvation would never be completed. But because it is up to Him, our salvation can never not be completed!

Paul finishes this thought by telling us that God will perform this work of salvation in us *"until the day of Jesus Christ."* This is a reference to the Rapture when God gathers all of His own to Himself. It is, in sports vernacular, all the way until the final whistle blows and all the time is drained off the clock, and we are in the locker room celebrating the victory.

If you are saved and want to know how secure your salvation is, it is as secure as if you had already gotten to heaven yesterday and were now busily decorating your mansion.

Paul now arrives in this section of verses at the point that leads me to call them "the glow."

Philippians 1:7 *Even as it is meet for me to think this of you all, because I have you in my heart; inasmuch as both in my bonds, and in the defence and confirmation of the gospel, ye all are partakers of my grace.*

Please believe me when I tell you that these were not exactly "standard fare words" for Paul. Referring back to what he said of them in the previous verse, the fact that he knew they were saved and forever saved, Paul begins verse seven by saying, "*It is meet for me to think this of you all.*" That phrase simply means that it is an appropriate and right thought. But it is the next phrase, the "because," that is so unusual. Paul said, in so many words, "It is right for me to believe that the God who has begun your salvation and is maintaining your salvation will fully complete your salvation... because I love you with all of my heart."

Be honest; does that not sound like a case of theological whiplash? It almost sounds like he has gone straight from Schaefer's Systematic Theology to a Hallmark card! And in case you are wondering, those words "I have you in my heart" only occur this one time in the entire Bible!

So why is it that Paul did not say something like, "It is right for me to believe that the God who has begun your salvation and is maintaining your salvation will fully complete your salvation because that is pure and proper doctrine and theology"? Why did he instead say, "It is right for me to believe that the God who has begun your salvation and is maintaining your salvation will fully complete your salvation... because I love you with all of my heart"?

To begin with, please understand that Paul was not at all basing his doctrine on his feelings. Rather, he was stipulating the doctrine that he had already stated and then telling them why it personally meant so much to him. He was taking an academic subject and making it personal because, to him, it truly was. Remember, this entire book of Philippians was precipitated by an emotion, that of joy. Simply put, Paul very dearly loved these people; he was thrilled that they were saved, and he viewed it as appropriate to believe what he believed about them because they were saved, and he loved them.

He moves from there in the first part of verse seven, though, to once again giving some of the why of his love for them, saying, "*inasmuch as both in my bonds, and in the defence and confirmation of the gospel, ye all are partakers of my grace.*"

One of the reasons Paul so loved them was that when he was in chains and when he stood before hostile crowds defending and confirming the gospel message, they were partakers of his grace in all of that. This is another reference to the fact that once they got saved, they determined to get the gospel to the rest of the world as well, and they supported Paul to make that happen. They became "partakers of his grace." Every soul that Paul won was pure grace, the gift of God. And the Philippians, by investing in Paul, shared in that grace! If we can put it in financial terms, because they invested in what Paul was doing, part of the dividends went to them.

You and I may never make it to a foreign field with the gospel. But if we invest in the missionaries who do, part of their spiritual dividends go to us.

You may never pastor a church and stand and preach the gospel to a congregation and visitors week after week. But if you invest in the church and pastor who do, part of their spiritual dividends go to you.

Philippians 1:8 *For God is my record, how greatly I long after you all in the bowels of Jesus Christ.*

These words in verse eight tie back to the words "I *have you in my heart*" of verse seven. So look at those two phrases together to understand what Paul was saying here:

"...because I have you in my heart; For God is my record, how greatly I long after you all in the bowels of Jesus Christ."

Once again, the master of New Testament theological doctrine, Paul the Apostle, becomes utterly emotional in these words. When he said, *"For God is my record,"* it meant the same thing as when we say, "You are my witness!" Paul was telling them that he would not be ashamed to call God Himself as a witness of all that he was saying about how much he loved them.

The entire closing phrase goes this way, *"For God is my record, how greatly I long after you all in the bowels of Jesus Christ."*

When we in our day tell someone, "I long for you," we are expressing the same sentiment that Paul expressed when he used the words, *"How greatly I long after you all."* But unlike what we would say, he added, *"in the bowels of Jesus Christ."*

Clearly, Paul did not have in mind what we think of in medical or anatomical terms when we use the word "bowels." What people in his day meant by that word was "the deepest emotions, the heart." So Paul was telling them that he longed after them with the very same heartbeat that Jesus Christ Himself longed for them.

Paul really did have these precious people in his heart. And in that, he sets an example for every one of us. All of us should love our brothers and sisters in Christ, our forever family, exactly like that.

Chapter Two
A Beautiful Set of Bookends

Philippians 1:9 *And this I pray, that your love may abound yet more and more in knowledge and in all judgment;* **10** *That ye may approve things that are excellent; that ye may be sincere and without offence till the day of Christ;* **11** *Being filled with the fruits of righteousness, which are by Jesus Christ, unto the glory and praise of God.* **12** *But I would ye should understand, brethren, that the things which happened unto me have fallen out rather unto the furtherance of the gospel;* **13** *So that my bonds in Christ are manifest in all the palace, and in all other places;* **14** *And many of the brethren in the Lord, waxing confident by my bonds, are much more bold to speak the word without fear.* **15** *Some indeed preach Christ even of envy and strife; and some also of good will:* **16** *The one preach Christ of contention, not sincerely, supposing to add affliction to my bonds:* **17** *But the other of love, knowing that I am set for the defence of the gospel.*

In the first eight verses, Paul expressed to the Philippians how much joy they brought him each time he thought of them and that he thanked God for them each and every time he prayed for them. And now, in this second section of verses, he continues to talk about praying for them. But he also uses the same word twice as bookends, as it were, to the thought he wants to convey. Notice how he starts and closes these verses:

Philippians 1:9 *And this I pray, that your* **love** *may abound yet more and more in knowledge and in all judgment;*

Philippians 1:17 *But the other of* **love**, *knowing that I am set for the defence of the gospel.*

Let's get into these verses and see what these two bookends hold.

A place for love

Philippians 1:9 *And this I pray, that your love may abound yet more and more in knowledge and in all judgment;* **10** *That ye may approve things that are excellent; that ye may be sincere and without offence till the day of Christ;* **11** *Being filled with the fruits of righteousness, which are by Jesus Christ, unto the glory and praise of God.*

Paul began by praying that the Philippians' love would abound. This is *agapay* love that he is referencing, the deep, self-sacrificial love for the benefit of another. There is no more profound type of love. In our day, when the word love is used, people usually think of it in a much cheaper way than how real love really is. Qurollo said it this way, "Love is not some sickening, sentimental feeling that is lightly expressed as it often is in the twenty-first century." (Qurollo)

If I may phrase it another way, real love is not candy; it is Calvary. Real love is something deep and profound and holy. That kind of love is what the Philippians had, and Paul wanted them to have even more of it. The word abound is from *perissuay,* and it means "to exceed a fixed number." In other words, think something like, "I want your love to be so big that it cannot be quantified or measured."

When you see this, the temptation is to imagine some ooey-gooey version of love that ignores all sin and wrong and just accepts everyone and everything. And that is what makes the next few qualifying phrases so jarring:

Philippians 1:9 *And this I pray, that your love may abound yet more and more* **in knowledge** *and* **in all judgment;**

Knowledge and judgment are generally not words that we put in the same sentence as love. But here, in a sentence where Paul is praying for their love to be so big that it cannot be measured or quantified, he then says, *"**in knowledge** and **in all judgment**."* There are a few different ways to express knowledge in the language our English New Testament came from. This particular one is *epignosei*, and it means "a full, complete knowledge and recognition." It is a knowledge that does not hide its face from flaws and errors and pretend they are not there. Judgment, in this verse, is from *aisthaysai,* and it means "perception and discernment in moral matters." So tie all of that together and let what Paul was saying sink in. He wanted their love to be without measure in fully knowing and understanding things and in making proper discerning judgments between them.

This is the way God views love. Any so-called love that turns a blind eye to sin and wrong, any so-called love that either places sin and righteousness on an equal level or, worse still, makes sin out to be superior to righteousness, is not real love at all! Consider the main issue of the modern age, "sexual expression." People drive around in traffic with rainbow-colored bumper stickers saying, "Love Is Love," and by that, they mean, "How dare you judge anyone for being homosexual or polyamorous or a pedophile!" But the fact of the matter is that real love is trying to rescue people from hell, not helping them to be more comfortable with their sin on the way there. Real love is telling the truth about sin so that others will not be tempted to go that way rather than having parades to make it look enticing to the innocent.

Mind you, though, real love is also telling the truth in love, not telling people they are going to hell and sounding like you are looking forward to seeing it happen.

Philippians 1:10 *That ye may approve things that are excellent; that ye may be sincere and without offence till the day of Christ;*

Paul is still continuing the thought of real love in verse ten. And as he does, he quickly comes to a word that is, again, a very popular word today, the word "approve." If you ever weigh in on matters of sexual choice and expression, you will very quickly find that you are expected to approve and even celebrate whatever anyone says or does. But Paul here said that real love is to approve the things that are excellent! The word excellent means "the things that are worth more, the things that are superior." It is clear, then, that Paul is still thinking in terms of that utterly hated word, "judgment." Paul wanted his beloved Philippians to discern the truth, figure out which things were moral and which things were immoral, and approve the better of those things, meaning the things that are moral.

God wants us to truly love purity. He wants us to approve the things that are right in His sight, not the things that are currently in vogue with the present wicked world.

He closes verse ten by saying, *"that ye may be sincere and without offence till the day of Christ;"* These, like the phrases before them, largely mean the opposite of how the world views and uses them. The word "sincere" is from *eilikrinays,* and it means "pure and unmixed." Real love does not open the arms and welcome in filthiness. Real love keeps itself pure, righteous only, with no admixture of sin. It is when we come to the phrase "without offense," though, that the wicked world will pounce, and even many carnal Christians will haughtily proclaim that the most important thing on earth is that we never say or do anything to offend the lost. But this word is from *aproskopoi,* and it means "blameless, undamaged, not causing to stumble."

28

As with what we saw earlier, these are moral terms, not fuzzy feelings. And this does not refer to how the lost world views us, but to how God the righteous judge views us! That is why the last phrase of verse ten says *"till the day of Christ"* instead of "till the world likes us." This points ahead to the day that Christ will judge the world:

Acts 17:31 *Because he hath appointed a day, in the which he will judge the world in righteousness by that man whom he hath ordained; whereof he hath given assurance unto all men, in that he hath raised him from the dead.*

We will all stand before God either at the Judgment Seat of Christ or the Great White Throne. Real love will have us standing before God blameless; false love will have us standing before God either losing rewards or forever condemned. Further elaborating on this, verse eleven says:

Philippians 1:11 *Being filled with the fruits of righteousness, which are by Jesus Christ, unto the glory and praise of God.*

Real love will have us filled, not with opinion or emotion, but with the fruits of righteousness. In other words, a philosophy of life produces fruits of some kind. A right philosophy of life, a philosophy of life that comes from Scripture and therefore pleases God, will produce righteousness in us, not tolerance for sin. And, while Paul is often falsely accused of contradicting sweet, sweet Jesus, we find here that these fruits of righteousness are actually produced by Jesus Christ and bring glory and praise to God. Here is how Jesus Himself said much the same thing:

Matthew 7:20 *Wherefore by their fruits ye shall know them.* **21** *Not every one that saith unto me, Lord, Lord, shall enter into the kingdom of heaven; but he that doeth the will of my Father which is in heaven.* **22** *Many will say to me in that day, Lord, Lord, have we not prophesied in thy name? and in thy name have cast out devils? and in thy name done many* *wonderful works? 23 And then will I profess unto them, I never knew you: depart from me, ye that work iniquity.*

As you can see, there is not a millimeter of difference between Jesus' view and Paul's view on this subject. Real love produces and promotes holiness, and a life lived in iniquity will never be pleasing to God.

A purpose for trials

Philippians 1:12 *But I would ye should understand, brethren, that the things which happened unto me have fallen out rather unto the furtherance of the gospel; 13 So that my bonds in Christ are manifest in all the palace, and in all other places;*

There is a pretty dramatic shift from the doctrinal to the personal at this point in the text. Paul has been talking about them and teaching them, but now he turns to himself. He wanted the Philippians to know why he was going through some severe difficulties. He called them "the things which have happened unto me." What were those things? Mainly the fact that he had undergone persecution and a murder attempt on his life, had to appeal to Caesar for a trial in Rome since he could not get a fair trial from the Jews, had suffered a shipwreck on the way there, and had now spent a significant amount of time incarcerated while literally having not broken a single law. But in spite of all of that, he was not bitter. And here, in his own words, is why:

"I would ye should understand, brethren, that the things which happened unto me have fallen out rather unto the furtherance of the gospel."

In other words, "I want you to understand that everything that has happened to me has resulted in the gospel getting to more and more and more people!" If your number one goal in life is to get the gospel out, then anything that happens to accomplish that can be viewed as a good thing, no matter how "bad" of a thing it is. And look in the next verse at who some of those people were:

Philippians 1:13 *So that my bonds in Christ are manifest in all the palace, and in all other places;*

Let that sink in. Paul being in bondage for Christ became known in Caesar's palace. And it did not just become "known" there, it did its job there:

Philippians 4:22 *All the saints salute you, chiefly they that are of Caesar's household.*

People in Caesar's household heard the gospel from Paul and got saved! And when you know who that "Caesar" was, it makes it all the more remarkable. Listen to what Adam Clarke said of this:

"Nero was at this time emperor of Rome: a more worthless, cruel, and diabolic wretch never disgraced the name or form of man; yet in his family there were Christians." (508)

We will meet and speak to people in Nero's family in heaven because of what Paul went through. Can you imagine any other circumstance under which they would ever even hear of the gospel? Do you imagine for even a moment that Paul would have been able simply to travel to Rome, knock on the door of the palace and say, "Hi, I'm Paul, I'm from the church down the road, and I just wanted to talk to you for a few moments about Jesus..."

Not. A. Chance. The only way in the world he would ever get inside the palace with the gospel is to be brought there in chains.

A paradox of love

Philippians 1:14 *And many of the brethren in the Lord, waxing confident by my bonds, are much more bold to speak the word without fear.* **15** *Some indeed preach Christ even of envy and strife; and some also of good will:* **16** *The one preach Christ of contention, not sincerely, supposing to add affliction to my bonds:* **17** *But the other of love, knowing that I am set for the defence of the gospel.*

31

By this time in the life of the early church, Paul was the most well-known preacher on earth. When a man like that goes to prison for preaching, it causes shock waves, and it also produces ripple effects. And it certainly did in this case. When Paul went to Rome in chains for the gospel, some other believers found their spines and their voices. People who had been timid about speaking up for Christ suddenly decided that if he was willing to be tried and even to die for the gospel, they should be brave about it, too. They actually lost their fear and started speaking up as if they were Paul himself! God has never invested all of the work in one man; the work of the church rises and falls on all of us, not on any one of us.

In verse fifteen, though, Paul let the Philippians in on a bit of a paradoxical situation in all of this:

Philippians 1:15 *Some indeed preach Christ even of envy and strife; and some also of good will:*

The first part of this verse is truly hard to even wrap the mind around. Mind you, the words are simple enough, but the situation itself is just mind-boggling. There were literally people preaching Christ out of a motivation of envy and strife! They viewed Paul as a rival, not as a fellow laborer. In his imprisonment, they saw an opportunity to "grow their own congregations!" These men, whoever they were, became very good indicators of what a lot of preachers would be like for the next couple of thousand years. But the trap in this is that we often come to think that all preachers are like that when they are not. Look again at how the verse ends:

"and some also of good will:"

Yes, there were some preaching at that moment with a really sick motivation, desiring to draw followers away from Paul and to themselves. But there were others who were preaching the gospel of "good will," meaning with absolutely the right motive. They loved God, they loved Paul, and they loved sinners and wanted to see them rescued from hell. How very different those two kinds of people are!

Look at how he describes those two groups more fully in the final two verses:

Philippians 1:16 *The one preach Christ of contention, not sincerely, supposing to add affliction to my bonds:* **17** *But the other of love, knowing that I am set for the defence of the gospel.*

"The one" in verse sixteen refers back to the first set of preachers in the last verse, those who preached Christ "of envy and strife." These people are described in verse sixteen as preaching out of contention, not out of a sincere heart. In doing what they were doing, they actually hoped to make Paul more miserable in his bondage.

Now, what you need to understand about people like that is that, in purely theological terms, they are horse's rear ends.

It would be nice to think that no people of such poor character are even in the ministry. It would also be foolish to think that no people of such poor character are even in the ministry. But what Paul's adversaries, in this instance, did not understand is the mistake that they were making. And by mistake, I mean that if they intended to make Paul miserable, the only way they could have done so is to contradict the preaching of Christ. But by actually preaching Christ, even though they were jerks, the message was still getting out there, and that is all Paul cared about. That says a lot, by the way, about Paul's character. And it also sets a pretty high bar for anyone in the ministry today.

But in stark contrast to those pathetic and putrid preachers, look at the other side of the paradox in verse seventeen:

Philippians 1:17 *But the other of love, knowing that I am set for the defence of the gospel.*

If the first phrase of verse seventeen seems to be missing a verb, it is because the verb was supplied in verse sixteen, namely the phrase "preach Christ," or as we would put it in our modern vernacular, "is preaching Christ." So, while the southern end of the northern bound horses were preaching Christ out of contention, there was a different group entirely that was preaching Christ out of love. And that love was born out of the knowledge that Paul was *"set for the defense of the gospel."*

That phrase contains a pretty interesting word within it. *"The defense"* is from the word *apologia,* and we get our word apologetics from it. It means "a verbal defense, a reasoned statement or argument." Paul did not just preach the gospel; he also very thoroughly and systematically verbally defended it. He did not just say, "The gospel is that Jesus lived and died and was buried and rose again," he proved it as a lawyer would prove a case in court. He knew and could quote all of the Old Testament Scripture regarding it. He knew all the contemporary evidence for it. He could point to all of the witnesses who saw it.

As this verse points out, Paul was not just going to do it, he knew that he was "set" for it, meaning that this was his purpose, and he would not back away from it under any circumstances. One of the results of that was not just that people got saved, even people as important as those in Nero's household, but also that other preachers loved him for it and stepped up to do it for him when he was imprisoned and could not do it himself out in the public square any longer.

This section of verses begins with love, mainly with Paul's prayer that their love would increase and that, therefore, they would always live right, and it ends with love, specifically the fact that some other preachers loved him enough to continue preaching to the public when he could not.

People often do what they do for Christ out of a sense of duty. And while we should feel a sense of duty to Christ, the fact of the matter is duty is nowhere near as long-lasting a motivation as love.

You may not always live right or spread the gospel based on the *duty* that you feel to Christ. But you will never have the *love* that you ought to have for Him and not live right or not spread the gospel.

Chapter Three
To Be (Here) or Not to Be

Philippians 1:18 *What then? notwithstanding, every way, whether in pretence, or in truth, Christ is preached; and I therein do rejoice, yea, and will rejoice.* **19** *For I know that this shall turn to my salvation through your prayer, and the supply of the Spirit of Jesus Christ,* **20** *According to my earnest expectation and my hope, that in nothing I shall be ashamed, but that with all boldness, as always, so now also Christ shall be magnified in my body, whether it be by life, or by death.* **21** *For to me to live is Christ, and to die is gain.* **22** *But if I live in the flesh, this is the fruit of my labour: yet what I shall choose I wot not.* **23** *For I am in a strait betwixt two, having a desire to depart, and to be with Christ; which is far better:* **24** *Nevertheless to abide in the flesh is more needful for you.* **25** *And having this confidence, I know that I shall abide and continue with you all for your furtherance and joy of faith;* **26** *That your rejoicing may be more abundant in Jesus Christ for me by my coming to you again.* **27** *Only let your conversation be as it becometh the gospel of Christ: that whether I come and see you, or else be absent, I may hear of your affairs, that ye stand fast in one spirit, with one mind striving together for the faith of the gospel;* **28** *And in nothing terrified by your adversaries: which is to them an evident token of perdition, but to you of salvation, and that of*

God. **29** *For unto you it is given in the behalf of Christ, not only to believe on him, but also to suffer for his sake;* **30** *Having the same conflict which ye saw in me, and now hear to be in me.*

In the last section of verses, Paul used love as beautiful bookends and dealt with knowledge and judgment, told them why he was undergoing such trials, let them know that the gospel had made it all the way into Nero's palace, and talked a bit about preachers who had sprung up in his absence, some of which had pure motives, and some of which had very impure motives. And as personal as all of that was, he will get more personal still in these verses as he bares his heart to the Philippians about whether he should live or die if given that choice.

A confidence of delivery

Philippians 1:18 *What then? notwithstanding, every way, whether in pretence, or in truth, Christ is preached; and I therein do rejoice, yea, and will rejoice.*

As the last section of verses came to a close, Paul was discussing two distinctly different groups of preachers that had arisen in his physical absence during his imprisonment. One of those groups was very sincere in their preaching of Christ; they loved Paul, and they loved the Christ that Paul was preaching. The other group, though, was preaching Christ out of contention. Their motive was to draw followers away from Paul, to have more converts than Paul, to have a bigger ministry than Paul. And Paul's response to that as verse eighteen begins is, *"What then?"* And if you have ever said the words "So what?" then you were expressing what Paul is expressing here.

Paul was utterly unbothered by what they were doing because, bad motivation or not, people were actually hearing the gospel! The way he expressed that feeling here was, *"notwithstanding, every way, whether in pretence, or in truth, Christ is preached; and I therein do rejoice, yea, and will rejoice.*" He was genuinely thrilled that people who hated his guts were preaching Christ and seeing people get saved.

Philippians 1:19 *For I know that this shall turn to my salvation through your prayer, and the supply of the Spirit of Jesus Christ,*

In ascertaining what Paul meant by these words, we can safely start by eliminating what it does not mean, namely salvation in the sense of being born again. Paul was unquestionably saved, converted to Christ, so that is not at all what he meant.

Please remember that Paul was right then in prison and on trial for his life. So when he speaks here of his salvation, he is talking about being saved from death at that time, being delivered from his bondage and set free. But in a way, that makes things all the more interesting when you notice how he started this verse, *"For I know that this shall turn to my salvation."* The "this" that he was referring to was those putrid preachers who were trying to cause him anguish by preaching Christ while he was behind bars. So, how exactly would that turn to his salvation, his deliverance from prison and death?

Look at the last phrase of the verse again for the explanation to that:

"through your prayer, and the supply of the Spirit of Jesus Christ,"

Here is the progression of thought. One, Paul was in prison and suffering. Two, people who hated him were preaching to try to make things worse for him. Three, Paul was telling the Philippians about that. Four, the Philippians were going to pray to the Father about that. Five, the Spirit of Jesus Christ, the Holy Spirit, was going to take that message to the Father. Six, the Father was then going to deliver Paul because of all of that.

Isn't it nice to know that the Father notices when people try to gouge His children and often simply turns their efforts at destruction into delivery?

Philippians 1:20 *According to my earnest expectation and my hope, that in nothing I shall be ashamed, but that with all boldness, as always, so now also Christ shall be magnified in my body, whether it be by life, or by death.*

Have you ever said something like, "Well, I know that thus and so is going to happen. But if the other happens instead, no big deal." That is the thought arc of verse twenty. In verse nineteen, Paul spoke of being confident of his delivery. But here, in verse twenty, he said much the same thing that the three Hebrew boys said when standing before King Nebuchadnezzar on the brink of the fiery furnace, "God can and will deliver us, but if not…"

Paul had what he calls here an *"earnest expectation and my hope, that in nothing I shall be ashamed,"* What he called an *earnest expectation* is what we would call a fondest desire and confident expectation. And it was specifically that *"in nothing I shall be ashamed."* And if we did not have the last half of the verse, we might assume that he was saying that he would be embarrassed if he did end up dying for the cause of Christ. But the last half of the verse, *"but that with all boldness, as always, so now also Christ shall be magnified in my body, whether it be by life, or by death"* clearly tells us that the only thing Paul would be embarrassed about was by not glorifying Christ in his living or in his dying. This was a situation of "If I live and stand for Christ, I am not ashamed, and if I die while standing for Christ, I am not ashamed. I will only ever be ashamed if I stop standing for Christ in life or in death!"

Before we move on, though, pay a bit of attention to the phrase *"magnified in my body."* With those four words, Paul puts much of modern so-called Christianity to shame. The carnal iteration of Christianity of our day, a "Christianity" that supposedly glorifies Christ with their spirit and with their worship and with their thoughts and with their feelings while their bodies dress immodestly and do not faithfully attend church and curse and drink and fornicate would make Paul vomit.

Real Christianity glorifies God in our bodies.

A choice of delight

Philippians 1:21 *For to me to live is Christ, and to die is gain.*

Paul was a pretty logical thinker. As such, he knew that he was either going to live or die, and neither of those things was his choice. But he knew that he did have a choice as to how to respond to either of those potentialities. And the choice he made was to delight in either one, thus producing a "win either way" result.

Paul's said that, to him, to live is Christ. By that, he meant that he regarded Christ as the very reason for living. But he then said that, to him, to die is gain. And by that, he meant that he would obviously gain tremendously by dying. His battered and constantly aching body would be made new, he would no longer be in chains, he would be able to see clearly again, he would never be beaten or shipwrecked or snake bit or stoned again, and he would finally get to see Jesus face to face.

And if you are born again as he was, you can look at things the exact same way. You can make Christ your very reason for living and, therefore, look forward to every day. And you can understand that dying simply takes you to heaven and, therefore, view death as a gain rather than a loss.

A clear decision

Philippians 1:22 *But if I live in the flesh, this is the fruit of my labour: yet what I shall choose I wot* [know] *not.*

The wording of this verse is a bit odd to our Western minds, but Paul was basically saying that if he lives, his life will still produce fruit, specifically labor for Christ. But if he could choose, he does not know which he would choose, life or death.

41

Think about that for just a moment. How many of us would even regard that as a question? It just seems automatic for us to choose to go on living. But Paul so loved Christ that it was a very real conundrum for him when he considered which one he wanted more!

Philippians 1:23 *For I am in a strait betwixt two, having a desire to depart, and to be with Christ; which is far better:* **24** *Nevertheless to abide in the flesh is more needful for you.*

The word "strait" means something akin to "pressed and distressed. We speak often in our vernacular of being between a rock and a hard place. But the opening phrase of verse twenty-three, "I am in a strait betwixt two," was more of an "I am between a gold mine and a diamond mine" situation that Paul was so distressed about. Remember, he saw no bad options here; living was Christ, and dying would be gain.

Paul wanted, most of all, to depart and be with Christ. He regarded it as "far better." And in those words, "depart and be with Christ," we find a doctrinal truth that drives a dagger into the heart of the heresy known as soul sleep. Paul was not going to take a long nap when his head came off; he was going to be with Christ. But even though he knew that was the case, he followed that up with the words of verse twenty-four, *"Nevertheless to abide in the flesh is more needful for you."* This was not pride or arrogance on the part of Paul. He really did have a huge impact on the Philippians, and he did not regard it as boasting to say so. It was merely the truth; if he lived, they would benefit from his continued teaching and preaching and writing and praying.

That, by the way, should be true of every believer. If we live, others should benefit spiritually because we do.

Philippians 1:25 *And having this confidence, I know that I shall abide and continue with you all for your furtherance and joy of faith;* **26** *That your rejoicing may be more abundant in Jesus Christ for me by my coming to you again.*

What Paul meant by these words was that, since it was indeed more needful for them that he live, he was confident that he would live and be released, at least for a while longer, and get to continue to minister to them, and that they would rejoice even more in Christ when it happened.

Paul was in bonds when he wrote these words. There was no indication that he would be released when he wrote these words. It was very abnormal for Rome to release people, especially under Nero, when he wrote these words. And yet, after two years of bondage in Rome, he was indeed released and continued to minister for a little while longer!

A conversation directed

Philippians 1:27 *Only let your conversation be as it becometh the gospel of Christ: that whether I come and see you, or else be absent, I may hear of your affairs, that ye stand fast in one spirit, with one mind striving together for the faith of the gospel;*

Paul has been writing about himself to the Philippians, and now he turns his attention to the Philippians themselves and what he expects of them no matter what happens to him. He began with the words, *"Only let your conversation be as it becometh the gospel of Christ."* As is commonly the case, this word "conversation" means much more than just talking; it indicated an entire manner of living and often referred to citizenship. God expects us to live our lives in a way that is becoming, appropriate for, the gospel of Christ. And since the gospel is the death, burial, and resurrection of Christ, that is a high bar indeed. Anything we do that is unworthy of people who have received such a gift is unbecoming of us.

Paul followed that thought up by saying, *"that whether I come and see you, or else be absent, I may hear of your affairs, that ye stand fast in one spirit, with one mind striving together for the faith of the gospel;"*

Whether he ended up living or dying, whether he got to come and see them again or never saw them again, he wanted to hear that they were standing fast in one spirit, with one mind striving together for the faith of the gospel. In simple terms, he wanted them to be getting along with each other and working well together. And the reason he wanted this was "for the faith of the gospel." Think of it this way: he wanted them all on the same page and rowing the same direction for the purpose of spreading the faith of the gospel of Christ.

Philippians 1:28 *And in nothing terrified by your adversaries: which is to them an evident token of perdition, but to you of salvation, and that of God.*

The "and" that begins this verse tells us that the instruction of the last verse is still ongoing. Not only does Paul want them standing together and working well together, he wants them all to not be terrified by their adversaries in anything. And this introduces a new fact to us in this epistle, namely that the Philippians were undergoing persecution. Clearly, this is not a surprising thing since Paul himself was brutally persecuted while there. And the Paul who was not terrified by the adversaries in Philippi, wanted the Philippians themselves not to be terrified by them.

In the last phrase of this verse, *"which is to them an evident token of perdition, but to you of salvation, and that of God,"* the "which is to them" means "as far as they are concerned," and "token" means "evidence." So the entire thought runs like this: "The fact that you are being persecuted is, as far as your adversaries are concerned, proof that they are headed for perdition. But the fact that you are being persecuted is, as far as you are concerned, proof that you have been saved by God."

Examining which side of the persecution line a person is on when it comes to the gospel is an incredibly solid way to determine whether people are heading for heaven or hell. Those who persecute the ones who are preaching the gospel are giving evidence of being lost, and those who are persecuted for preaching the gospel are giving evidence of being saved.

Philippians 1:29 *For unto you it is given in the behalf of Christ, not only to believe on him, but also to suffer for his sake;* **30** *Having the same conflict which ye saw in me, and now hear to be in me.*

Imagine, if you will, a thirtieth birthday party. Banners hang from the ceiling, helium balloons are tied to strings, and everyone is wearing party hats. And then, several large men come in and say, "And now, time for your gift!" and proceed to beat the "birthday boy" into a coma. To put it mildly, that would be considered an odd gift. But in verse twenty-nine, Paul told the Philippians, *"For unto you it is **given** in the behalf of Christ, not only to believe on him, but also to suffer for his sake."* Given means "to be graciously bestowed as a gift." the Philippians had legitimately been given the gift, not only of believing on Christ but also of suffering for Christ.

We tend to think of that the exact opposite way, do we not? We tend to think that some people "have to suffer for Christ," when the truth of the matter is that some people "get to suffer for Christ!" Mind you, there is nothing in our flesh that desires that, but it is a gracious gift nonetheless, whether desired or not. Everyone gets to say, "Christ suffered for me," but seemingly only a select few get to say, "I suffered for Christ."

To the Philippians, this was not a foreign concept since, as Paul observed in verse thirty, *"Having the same conflict which ye saw in me, and now hear to be in me."* They saw him suffer for Christ while he was there with them in Philippi, and now they were hearing about him suffering for Christ during his imprisonment in Rome.

To be (here) or not to be. For Paul, that really was the question. But since he viewed living as Christ and dying as gain, he was going to be a winner either way. And that is a fantastic pattern of life for us to emulate.

Chapter Four
Mind Matters

Philippians 2:1 *If there be therefore any consolation in Christ, if any comfort of love, if any fellowship of the Spirit, if any bowels and mercies,* **2** *Fulfil ye my joy, that ye be likeminded, having the same love, being of one accord, of one mind.* **3** *Let nothing be done through strife or vainglory; but in lowliness of mind let each esteem other better than themselves.* **4** *Look not every man on his own things, but every man also on the things of others.* **5** *Let this mind be in you, which was also in Christ Jesus:* **6** *Who, being in the form of God, thought it not robbery to be equal with God:* **7** *But made himself of no reputation, and took upon him the form of a servant, and was made in the likeness of men:* **8** *And being found in fashion as a man, he humbled himself, and became obedient unto death, even the death of the cross.* **9** *Wherefore God also hath highly exalted him, and given him a name which is above every name:* **10** *That at the name of Jesus every knee should bow, of things in heaven, and things in earth, and things under the earth;* **11** *And that every tongue should confess that Jesus Christ is Lord, to the glory of God the Father.*

In the last section of verses, Paul bared his heart to the Philippians about his emotional conundrum; he wanted to go home to be with Jesus, but he knew the Philippians still needed him. And his conclusion, based on that, was that God was going to let him live a little while longer.

As chapter two begins, Paul will deal with matters of the mind.

A mind for others

Philippians 2:1 *If there be therefore any consolation in Christ, if any comfort of love, if any fellowship of the Spirit, if any bowels and mercies,* **2** *Fulfil ye my joy, that ye be likeminded, having the same love, being of one accord, of one mind.*

Before we begin to break down the words and phrases, just take note of the entirety of Paul's words in these two verses. What you should immediately notice is that this is an incredibly emotional appeal. In one sentence, Paul used the words consolation, comfort of love, fellowship, bowels and mercies, joy, and love. So he is being unashamedly and overwhelmingly emotional in his plea to them in these verses.

Is there anything wrong with that? Certainly not. God made us emotional creatures, not living mathematical equations. In fact, look at who else used a very emotional appeal:

John 14:15 *If ye love me, keep my commandments.*

That was Jesus. Both Jesus and Paul made liberal usage of emotional appeal. As long as what is being requested is right and proper, emotional appeal is every bit as valid and, oftentimes, far more effective than mere intellectual appeal.

The "therefore" near the beginning of verse one goes back to what Paul wrote of from verses twenty-seven through thirty of the previous chapter, the fact that people were suffering for Christ and that the Philippians saw and heard of Paul suffering for Christ on their behalf. So, look at the whole sentence again, and let's begin to examine what he was asking based on that.

Philippians 2:1 *If there be therefore any consolation in Christ, if any comfort of love, if any fellowship of the Spirit, if any bowels and mercies,* **2** *Fulfil ye my joy, that ye be likeminded, having the same love, being of one accord, of one mind.*

To begin with, let me explain that when Paul used the word "if" at the start of verse one, he used it much like we do when we use an "if" like a "since." We will say something like "If there is a God in heaven," not questioning it, but believing it and basing something upon it. So this if was not something that Paul doubted; it was something he was very sure of.

Consolation in Christ means encouragement and exhortation. So, the thought here runs along the lines of "If being in Christ has brought you help and encouragement, if it has made your days brighter."

Comfort of love means "comfort that has been produced in you by love." Christ loving them and Christians loving each other because of what Christ did had indeed brought them comfort. Fellowship of the Spirit refers to the Holy Spirit, and it means the fellowship that He Himself has with us as believers and the fellowship that He causes believers to have with each other. Believers get to experience both the wonder of God Himself in the person of the Holy Spirit fellowshipping with us and the joy of fellowshipping with each other because we have Him in common. There is nothing on earth quite like the local church in that regard. It is only in the local church that you will find people of different races and nationalities and cultures and backgrounds and socio-economic levels who pull for different teams and like different things having fellowship closer than that of flesh and blood family.

Bowels and mercies means something along the lines of "hearts and compassion."

So, using all that Paul said in verse one as the introduction to what he asks in verse two, what you have is "If being in Christ has brought you help and encouragement, if it has made your days brighter, if you have been comforted by the love of Christ, if you enjoy fellowshipping with the Holy Spirit and with each other, if you have any heart and compassion, *"Fulfil ye my joy, that ye be likeminded, having the same love, being of one accord, of one mind."*

Verse one is the basis; verse two is the request.

The request began with *"fulfil ye my joy."* That means, "You have already made me very happy, but please make me even more so; please make me unable to ever be any happier." And what would accomplish that for him is for them to be *"likeminded, having the same love, being of one accord, of one mind."* All of those phrases simply mean "genuinely getting along." You see, as wonderful as the Philippian church was, it was, like every church, made up of actual people. And just like in every church, some of those people were *not* getting along, and it was hindering what could be done for Christ. In chapter four, Paul will go so far as to mention two of those people by name! That was a pretty drastic thing, so it shows you how bad it had gotten and how desperately it needed to be dealt with.

Philippians 2:3 *Let nothing be done through strife or vainglory; but in lowliness of mind let each esteem other better than themselves.* **4** *Look not every man on his own things, but every man also on the things of others.*

These should legitimately be two of the most memorized verses on earth. I can think of no other verses that, if obeyed, would do more to ensure that churches always ran smoothly. But not just churches. The "nothing" in verse one clearly takes things beyond merely the local church. This "nothing" can and does apply equally well to marriage and the home and to all other human settings.

Paul began with, *"Let nothing be done through strife or vainglory."* Strife is from the word *eritheia*, and it means "selfish ambition, electioneering." Vainglory is from *kenodoxia,* and it means "vanity and conceit." Anything we do with the idea of gaining power for ourselves or to make ourselves look important to others or to draw attention to ourselves fits under these categories.

The hinge of the two phrases in this verse, "but," is once again from the strong adversative *alla.* Think of it like "but by extreme contrast" or "but way on the other side of things." So, the contrast to *"strife or vainglory"* is *"but in lowliness of mind let each esteem other better than themselves."*

This second phrase is the exact diametrical opposite of the first. *"In lowliness of mind"* means "with humility and modesty." *"Let each esteem other better than themselves"* is very much self-explanatory; in whatever we do, we must view the "others" around us as the important ones rather than ourselves.

No marriage ever disintegrates when both husband and wife obey that command. No church ever implodes when everyone in it obeys that command. No friendship ever dies when both parties obey that command.

Paul closes this section of thought with, *"Look not every man on his own things, but every man also on the things of others."* Once again, this is such an essential yet oft-ignored command. It simply means, "Stop just thinking of you and yours; pay attention to others, see things through their eyes, notice their needs, and act accordingly." And it is important for you to know which of the two common Greek words for "others" is used here. This is not *allos,* meaning "others of the same kind," it is *heteros,* meaning "others of a different kind." In other words, it is usually pretty easy to consider the wants and needs of "our circle," but this command is that we consider the wants and needs of those outside of our circle. Even in a church, there will be people we are closer to than others, especially as a church grows. And the only way that can ever work is by obeying this command.

A mind like Christ

Philippians 2:5 *Let this mind be in you, which was also in Christ Jesus:* **6** *Who, being in the form of God, thought it not robbery to be equal with God:* **7** *But made himself of no reputation, and took upon him the form of a servant, and was made in the likeness of men:* **8** *And being found in fashion as a man, he humbled himself, and became obedient unto death, even the death of the cross.*

These are the verses that I chose many years ago as my life verse. They are what I sign under my name in every Bible or book that I am asked to sign.

You will sometimes hear a very unusual and rarely used word associated with these and following verses, the word *kenosis*. If you ever hear that, be aware that it means "emptying." We will find that word in verse seven. Just know for now that if you hear of the Great Kenosis passage of Scripture, these are some of the verses that are being referenced.

This passage tells us how Christ thought and how we are, therefore, to think. That is what Paul means when he says, *"Let this mind be in you, which was also in Christ Jesus:"* in verse five. And then in verses six through eight. He explained what that thinking was like for Christ and should be like for us.

Verse six is a preface to the way Christ thought, a phrase that lets us know how amazing it was that Christ thought the way He did. It says, *"Who, being in the form of God, thought it not robbery to be equal with God:"* In other words, Christ was absolutely, fully God, even in form. Before He became flesh on earth, He was God in heaven. Not partially God, not a lesser God, but "equal with God," meaning with God the Father. For any of us to claim that would be robbery since it does not belong to us. But Christ was able to claim it without thinking it to be robbery because it was His; He owned it; He had every right to it. And that truth is used to show how shocking His thought process was while in flesh on earth.

That thought process begins with *"But made himself of no reputation."* "Made" in verse seven is where we get the word *kenosis* that I mentioned earlier, and as I said, it means to empty. In heaven, the angels of God worshipped Him incessantly; on earth, He allowed Himself to be viewed as "the carpenter's son."

We are to think the same way. We are not to claw and scratch for glory, even glory that we feel we deserve.

This is not an easy thing for us.

We have fantastic custodians now at the church I pastor, but in the early days, that was not quite the case. There was a lady that we hired for $25 a week to come in and clean the church. It was just 4,000 square feet, and all we asked was for her to vacuum the floor and take out the trash. It took about an hour. $25 an hour in 1998 was pretty good money! And yet, for six solid weeks, she made excuses as to why she could not make it. And then she made it for a few weeks and only did about half a job. And for all of that time, when she did not show up Dana and I quietly did all of it, and when she showed up and left half of it undone, we quietly did what she left. And truth be told, I was getting pretty ill about the entire thing.

And then, one day, in the prayer room, one of the men stood up and said, "I think we need to say a word about the cleaning of the church." In my mind, I thought, "Somebody noticed what we were doing after all!"

He proceeded, "It has looked amazing these past few weeks."

I grinned and bowed my head a bit sheepishly.

Then he said, "Sister so and so has really been doing a great job; let's double what we are giving her!"

I bit my tongue. Nearly in half...

It is not easy not to claw and scratch for glory, even glory that we feel we deserve. But if we are going to think like Christ, we cannot be glory-centric; we cannot strive to "make ourselves of reputation." This was part two of Christ's temptation in the wilderness, if you will remember. Had Christ indeed jumped off of the pinnacle of the temple and been caught midair by angels, He would have been an immediate superstar. But He said no. And then, time after time, as He did miracles, He said, "Tell no man."

He emptied Himself; He made Himself of no reputation.

The second thing we find in regard to the thinking of Christ is that He *"took upon him the form of a servant."*

He fed meals to hungry multitudes. He touched the lepers. And with only hours left to live, He washed the dirty feet of His men.

He. Washed. Feet.

We are to think like servants. No matter "how high we rise through the ranks" we are to think like servants. If you are in the pews, be a servant. If you are in the pulpit, be a servant. If the King thinks like a servant, the subjects should surely think like servants!

The next thing we read of His thinking was that He was *"made in the likeness of men."* This means very literally what it says. He looked like a human being. He was God, and yet for thirty-three years, the only time He ever allowed Himself to look like God was on the Mount of Transfiguration, with only three human witnesses. For thirty-three years, he looked absolutely normal. There was nothing in His appearance to draw attention to Himself. In fact, look at what Isaiah prophesied of Him:

Isaiah 53:2b *...he hath no form nor comeliness; and when we shall see him, there is no beauty that we should desire him.*

Not only did Jesus allow Himself to look like a human, He allowed Himself to look like an unattractive human. There was nothing about Him that would be described as beautiful or comely. He made sure that anyone who followed Him did so because of His word and works, not because of His looks.

What does that mean for our way of thinking? How does it apply to us? It obviously does not mean that we are to try to make ourselves ugly. Remember, He got to choose how tall He would be, and what color His eyes would be, and what shape His face would be, and how big His nose would be. We get to choose none of that.

What it does mean for us is that we should not think, "In what way can I dress and do my hair and fix my makeup to draw the most possible attention to myself? How garish can I be? How much can I stand out?" That type of thought process was utterly foreign to Christ and should be equally foreign to us.

Verse eight closes out the description of Christ's thinking by saying, "*And being found in fashion as a man, he humbled himself, and became obedient unto death, even the death of the cross.*"

You can rightly examine and apply the humility and the obedience either individually or as a package in this verse, either is valid, and neither does harm to the text. I tend to take it in package form; He humbled Himself, and as a result became obedient unto death."

The verse begins, though, with "*And being found in fashion as a man.*" This simply refers back to what was said in verse seven, "*and was made in the likeness of man.*" So, having robed Himself in flesh, Jesus "*humbled himself, and became obedient unto death, even the death of the cross.*"

Was Christ ever disobedient to His Father? Certainly not. But now He was asked to obey in something that He had never faced before, namely going to Calvary to suffer and die. And, faced with that brand new thing in which He had the choice to obey or disobey, He did as He always does and obeyed His Father yet again.

For us, the command of verse five then tells us that this is a command that we think obediently. Whatever is placed before us from day to day, even if it be painful to body or heart, we are simply to obey. That is the way Christ thought, and it is the way we are to think.

A marvelous outgrowth

When we read that pretty shocking list from verses one through eight of how we are to think, the very natural tendency of our flesh is to say, "But what about me?" God knew that. And rather than scolding such a thought, here is what He had Paul write next.

Philippians 2:9 *Wherefore God also hath highly exalted him, and given him a name which is above every name:* **10** *That at the name of Jesus every knee should bow, of things in heaven, and things in earth, and things under the earth;* **11** *And that every tongue should confess that Jesus Christ is Lord, to the glory of God the Father.*

Wherefore, meaning "Because He thought like He thought," God the Father highly exalted Jesus. The implication for us is that as we think like Christ, He will, in His time, highly exalt us as well!

Look, though, at exactly how He exalted Him because it says much about our dear Lord.

We first find that the Father has *"given him a name which is above every name."* At His birth, our Savior shockingly was given one of the most common names of His day, something no more unique than John would be in our day. And yet, because of how Christ thought, because He became obedient to the death of the cross, that name is now the most famous name in the whole of human history. The world may love His name or hate His name, but everyone knows His name, and no name has a bigger impact than His. And for eternity, His will be the name that is sung of and adored.

Verses ten and eleven close out that topic by saying, *"That at the name of Jesus every knee should bow, of things in heaven, and things in earth, and things under the earth; And that every tongue should confess that Jesus Christ is Lord, to the glory of God the Father."*

"That at the name of Jesus every knee should bow." Do not be thrown off by the word "should." In our day and vernacular, "should" generally implies a possibility but not a certainty. But there is no possibility found in this word; it is actually an utter certainty. It is from the word *kampsay,* and it means "to bow the knee." Here is how Paul put it when writing to the Romans:

Romans 14:11 *For it is written, As I live, saith the Lord, every knee shall bow to me, and every tongue shall confess to God.*

So, because Christ thought like He thought, the Father has given Him a name above every name, and every knee absolutely will bow to Him, *"of things in heaven, and things in earth, and things under the earth."*

Let that last phrase sink in; it encompasses the entire universe, most of which does not believe and will not receive Christ. It even includes those who are in hell for rejecting Christ, things *"under the earth."* At some point, every single knee will bow; they may never have had bowed hearts, but they will one and all bow the knee.

But not only will all bow the knee, verse eleven closes this out by saying, *"And that every tongue should confess that Jesus Christ is Lord, to the glory of God the Father."* Once again, the "should" does not imply a possibility; it introduces a certainty. Every tongue, even those who hated and rejected Christ, will one day acknowledge Him as Lord. And this will bring glory to God the Father who chose His Son to be such.

So, does how we think really matter? Yes, unquestionably. Thoughts produce actions, and actions bring either blessing or blistering from the Father.

If you want the blessings, do right. And if you want to do right so that you can have the blessings, train yourself to think right.

Chapter Five
Work Out Your Own Salvation

Philippians 2:12 *Wherefore, my beloved, as ye have always obeyed, not as in my presence only, but now much more in my absence, work out your own salvation with fear and trembling.* **13** *For it is God which worketh in you both to will and to do of his good pleasure.* **14** *Do all things without murmurings and disputings:* **15** *That ye may be blameless and harmless, the sons of God, without rebuke, in the midst of a crooked and perverse nation, among whom ye shine as lights in the world;* **16** *Holding forth the word of life; that I may rejoice in the day of Christ, that I have not run in vain, neither laboured in vain.* **17** *Yea, and if I be offered upon the sacrifice and service of your faith, I joy, and rejoice with you all.* **18** *For the same cause also do ye joy, and rejoice with me.*

Paul just finished writing to his beloved Philippians about "mind matters." How we think really does matter! And he will now segue from that into a very practical outgrowth, namely how what we believe on the inside is to be manifested to the world on the outside.

The ins and outs of salvation

Philippians 2:12 *Wherefore, my beloved, as ye have always obeyed, not as in my presence only, but now much more* *in my absence, work out your own salvation with fear and trembling.* **13** *For it is God which worketh in you both to will and to do of his good pleasure.*

The *"wherefore"* that begins this section of thought refers back to what was stated in verses ten and eleven, namely that every knee is going to bow before the Lord Jesus Christ, and every tongue is going to confess to Him. With this firmly in their view, Paul calls them beloved and tells them that *"as ye have always obeyed, not as in my presence only, but now much more in my absence, work out your own salvation with fear and trembling."*

The command is that they obey him now as they have always obeyed him before and work out their own salvation with the fear and trembling that comes from the understanding that Christ is the King of kings, and we must all answer to Him. But this phrase, *"work out your own salvation,"* has historically given rise to much error due to careless handling of the text and context of the verse.

If we were of a mind to do so, it would not be hard at all to come up with some very powerful yet very wrong illustrations of salvation. For instance:

"Imagine, if you will, a man who has fallen into a sinkhole near the ocean. No matter how hard he claws to get out, the walls are so soft and mushy that they continually cave in further as he frantically tries to do so. As his panic grows, he realizes in horror that water is starting to gather around his feet. The tide is coming in, and soon it will fill the entire hole and send him to his doom.

"But then he hears a voice calling down to him, 'Hello, sinner friend. It appears you've gotten yourself into quite a mess. But today is about to be the best day of your life because I'm here to rescue you. I'm going to put this ladder down into the pit; its name is Grace. It is very long and very hard to climb, but you can do it.'

"The ladder appeared over the edge and came down, down, down till it finally touched the bottom of the pit. And that man, using every ounce of effort and strength in his being, climbed that old ladder of grace and made his way safely onto solid ground..."

It would not be too hard to really dramatize that illustration and make it inspirational enough to have it end up on a greeting card! There is just one problem with it; it is absolutely unscriptural. Grace is not God handing us down the ladder so we can climb out of our pit; grace is God climbing down into the pit, coming down into the muck and mire where we are, and carrying us out. If we are having to "climb a ladder," then salvation has just stopped being produced by grace and has started being produced by works. But Paul said in **Romans 11:6**, *"And if by grace, then is it no more of works: otherwise grace is no more grace. But if it be of works, then is it no more grace: otherwise work is no more work."* In other words, it is either works or grace; those two things are completely different, and they don't go together.

Here is another thing people often say; in fact, many of my expensive commentaries say it. "God begins the process of our salvation by grace alone, but then we complete the process by our works." But again, look at what Scripture says:

Galatians 3:1 *O foolish Galatians, who hath bewitched you, that ye should not obey the truth, before whose eyes Jesus Christ hath been evidently set forth, crucified among you?* **2** *This only would I learn of you, Received ye the Spirit by the works of the law, or by the hearing of faith?* **3** *Are ye so foolish? having begun in the Spirit, are ye now made perfect by the flesh?*

The answer is "no." We have not "begun in the Spirit and yet are now made perfect by the flesh." It is all of grace, not of works.

Bible believers have understood and believed this for a long time. But then an interesting thing happens. We come to a passage like Philippians 2:12, and we read something that seems to throw a monkey wrench into what the rest of the Bible says about salvation:

Philippians 2:12 *Wherefore, my beloved, as ye have always obeyed, not as in my presence only, but now much more in my absence,* **_work out your own salvation_** *with fear and trembling.*

What in the world is going on here? Let me remind you, the man who wrote these words is the exact same man who wrote the words of **Ephesians 2:8-9**, *"For by grace are ye saved through faith; and that not of yourselves: it is the gift of God: Not of works, lest any man should boast."*

Has Paul forgotten from one letter to the next what he wrote? Is he really telling the Ephesians that salvation is by grace and then telling the Philippians that salvation is by works? What is this about?

Look at the very next verse, and you will begin to figure out this riddle.

Philippians 2:13 *For it is God which worketh in you both to will and to do of his good pleasure.*

We saw two words in Philippians 2:12 that seem very problematic, "work out." What two words do you see in Philippians 2:13 that look similar to those words in Philippians 2:12?

"Worketh in." We know that worketh means "works." So in verse twelve, we have *work out*, and in verse thirteen, we have *works in*. The word *work* in both verses is from the same Greek root word. But clearly, *out* and *in* are two very different words. Both of them in our language are words that denote location. We are "in here," not "out there." Keep that in mind, and let's look at this working in thing for a few minutes.

The subject at hand, according to verse twelve, is clearly salvation; there is absolutely no question about that. And in that context, Paul says in verse thirteen that it is God which works in us both to will and to do of His good pleasure. In other words, salvation is an internal thing, and God gets inside of us and produces it because it is His will and His good pleasure to do so. Salvation cannot be achieved from the outside in; it has to come from the inside out. So God goes to where we cannot go, gets all the way inside of us to the spirit and the soul, and produces salvation within us.

Now drop back to verse twelve again because now that we understand verse thirteen, it will not be hard for us to figure out the meaning of verse twelve.

Philippians 2:12 *Wherefore, my beloved, as ye have always obeyed, not as in my presence only, but now much more in my absence, work out your own salvation with fear and trembling.*

When we use the words "work it out" in our common everyday speech, it means that we are responsible for producing something or fixing something or doing something.

Little Bubba comes home and says, "Paw, I'm having trouble with Cletus; he keeps takin' my hog jowl lunch." And Paw says, "You better work it out, boy." Paw means that Bubba is responsible for producing a solution.

But we have already learned from verse thirteen that it is Christ who produces salvation in us. And we have learned from many, many verses of Scripture that our works cannot save us or help to save us.

But now that we know that the words "in and out" are words of location, and now that we know that Christ is doing the producing of salvation inside of us, we can figure out a very logical, different usage of the term "work out."

Here is what Paul is saying: it is Christ's task to produce salvation inside of us; it is our task to practice salvation outside of us.

Here is another way to put it that may make it make even more sense to you: it is up to Him to *give it*; it is up to us to *live it.* And you will not have to go far in the context of the passage to see that exact truth borne out:

Philippians 2:15 *That ye may be blameless and harmless, the sons of God, without rebuke, in the midst of a crooked and perverse nation, among whom ye shine as lights in the world;*

So the ins and outs of salvation are as follows: Christ produces it in us where the world cannot see it, and we live it outside of us where the world can see it.

The insistence on a right attitude

Philippians 2:14 *Do all things without murmurings and disputings:*

The first practical outgrowth Paul gives from the command to work out our own salvation is that we do all things without murmurings and disputings. This is another of many indications in this book that some of the Philippians were fighting like cats and dogs and that Paul wanted it to stop.

Murmurings is from the word *gongusmos,* and it means "complaining." Disputings is from the word *dialogismos*, and it means "arguments." And remember, please, this command is directed to people in a church!

People complaining is a very bad testimony for a church. People arguing is an incredibly bad testimony for a church. And yet, churches have an often well-earned stereotype as places of bawling and brawling.

It really ought to never be that way, if for no other reason, because this verse expressly forbids it. And remember that, in the context of what Paul is saying, it is forbidden because the world is watching, and we are to be working our inward salvation outwardly in front of them.

The influence of godliness

Philippians 2:15 *That ye may be blameless and harmless, the sons of God, without rebuke, in the midst of a crooked and perverse nation, among whom ye shine as lights in the world;*

Focus in on the first word of verse fifteen, the word "that." It directly ties to what came before it in verse fourteen; it is from the conjunction *hina,* and it means "in order that," or as we would say in common terms, "so that." So look at it with that definition tied to verse fourteen and leading into verse fifteen:

"Do all things without murmurings and disputings [so] *that ye may be blameless and harmless, the sons of God, without rebuke, in the midst of a crooked and perverse nation, among whom ye shine as lights in the world."*

This is what we mean about the influence of godliness, and it verifies exactly what I said in reference to verse fourteen. We are to make sure that the church is not a complaining and arguing body; we are to completely do away with bawlings and brawlings so that the outside world will see a good testimony in us.

The late Doug Marlette was an editorial cartoonist for the Charlotte Observer and the Atlanta Journal-Constitution. He was also the creator of the syndicated cartoon, Kudzu. It was basically about life in a small southern town. I have one of those Kudzu cartoons hanging up in my office. It shows a young man named Kudzu, along with his preacher, on a softball field. The preacher, in disgust, is saying to him, "This happens every time we play the Baptists. They squabble amongst themselves, and somebody winds up going off and forming a new team!"

The cartoon is hilarious but also a bit sad. That is the way the world views churches, not just Baptists, by the way, but churches in general, and often rightly so. But these verses tell us that we are to do all things without murmurings and disputings, no complaining and no arguing, so that we may be blameless and harmless, the sons of God, without rebuke, in the midst of a crooked and perverse nation, among whom we shine as lights in the world.

Blameless basically means "giving no legitimate occasion for others to accuse you of wrongdoing." Harmless means "pure, sincere, not deceptive." This is how to be viewed as sons of God, since the normal way of "the sons of men" is the exact opposite!

Without rebuke means "blameless, unblemished." It is once again an indication that there is no legitimate cause for accusation against us. And we are to live this complaint-free, no arguing, blameless, harmless, unblemished life in the very midst of "a crooked and perverse nation."

Ours certainly qualifies.

Crooked is from a unique word, the word *skolios*, we get our medical term scoliosis from it, which is where a person has a crooked spine. Our nation definitely has a crooked spine; America seemingly cannot even begin to stand up straight morally anymore. But we, the church, are to stand up straight morally in the midst of them.

Perverse is from the word *diastrepho,* and it means "distorted." Again, that is a perfectly accurate description of our nation which is now too distorted to know the difference between a man and a woman or even to be able to call child molestation evil. But we, the church, are to be undistorted on those and all other matters right in the midst of them. And the reason for all of this, as the end of verse fifteen makes clear, is because we are the ones tasked with shining as lights in the world. In thinking and in behavior, this world is becoming unbearably dark, and more so by the day. But the church is to behave in such a way in front of them that people who are crying out for light in the darkness will be able to see the light from us and make their way out of the darkness into the light.

Philippians 2:16 *Holding forth the word of life; that I may rejoice in the day of Christ, that I have not run in vain, neither laboured in vain.*

If the subject had ended at verse fifteen, people might be inclined to believe the error of lifestyle evangelism minus confrontational evangelism. In other words, "Just live like Christians in front of people and expect them to find their way to Christ." But the subject does not end in verse fifteen; it goes on into verse sixteen with the words "*Holding forth the word of life.*"

You see, it is not enough, ever, simply to live as a Christian. We are to be holding forth the word of life. Holding forth, from the word *epeko,* has a few different meanings. But the one that clearly fits this context is "to hold towards, to hold forth, to present." In other words, it is not enough for us to simply cling to the gospel privately for ourselves. We are to take that precious gift that we have been given and hold it out, present it to others so that they can have it as well.

An oft-used, Hallmarkesque quote goes, "Preach the gospel, and if necessary, use words."

And that makes for a great greeting card but terrible theology. Paul told us to hold forth the word of life specifically because just living it in front of people will never be enough.

Think about it. If we simply just live right in front of others, then people may assume that we are Christians. Or they may assume that we are just pretty nice people. Or they may assume that we had great parents who taught us right. Or they may assume that we are Buddhists or Hindus or any other of hundreds of different groups to teach general moral principles. So unless we are, along with living the Christian life, also verbally attributing that to Christ and telling others that He saved us and that is why we live the way we live, we are not fulfilling our responsibility as believers.

Look again at the last half of the verse to see how seriously Paul regarded this:

...that I may rejoice in the day of Christ, that I have not run in vain, neither laboured in vain.

As far as Paul was concerned, if the Philippian church was not both living as Christians in front of the world and preaching the gospel to the world, he would have nothing to rejoice about at the Judgment Seat of Christ in reference to his labor over them. If they were not both moral and evangelistic, he believed that his labor there in Philippi was completely in vain.

The "ifs" of sacrifice and joy

Philippians 2:17 *Yea, and if I be offered upon the sacrifice and service of your faith, I joy, and rejoice with you all.* **18** *For the same cause also do ye joy, and rejoice with me.*

When Paul said, "*Yea, and if I be offered upon the sacrifice and service of your faith,*" he meant, in our terms, "and if I do end up dying because I won you and other Gentiles to the Lord and trained you in the faith." Remember, when he wrote this letter to the Philippians, that was still a very real possibility.

So Paul was saying, "Even if I do die, as long as you all are living right and witnessing, I joy and rejoice with you all." And then, in verse eighteen, he acknowledges that the feelings are reciprocal; the Philippians think of him the exact same way.

How amazing is it that anyone could say and mean, "You know, I may die today for having told you about Jesus, but as long as I know that you all are actually living for Him and telling others how to be saved, my joy is absolutely as full as it can possibly be." But that is exactly how all of us ought to feel when we see believers not just making a profession, but actually "working out their own salvation."

Chapter Six
On the One Hand... And On the Other

Philippians 2:19 *But I trust in the Lord Jesus to send Timotheus shortly unto you, that I also may be of good comfort, when I know your state.* **20** *For I have no man likeminded, who will naturally care for your state.* **21** *For all seek their own, not the things which are Jesus Christ's.* **22** *But ye know the proof of him, that, as a son with the father, he hath served with me in the gospel.* **23** *Him therefore I hope to send presently, so soon as I shall see how it will go with me.* **24** *But I trust in the Lord that I also myself shall come shortly.* **25** *Yet I supposed it necessary to send to you Epaphroditus, my brother, and companion in labour, and fellowsoldier, but your messenger, and he that ministered to my wants.* **26** *For he longed after you all, and was full of heaviness, because that ye had heard that he had been sick.* **27** *For indeed he was sick nigh unto death: but God had mercy on him; and not on him only, but on me also, lest I should have sorrow upon sorrow.* **28** *I sent him therefore the more carefully, that, when ye see him again, ye may rejoice, and that I may be the less sorrowful.* **29** *Receive him therefore in the Lord with all gladness; and hold such in reputation:* **30** *Because for the work of Christ he was nigh unto death, not regarding his life, to supply your lack of service toward me.*

In the last section of verses, Paul explained that we have a responsibility based on what God has done inside of us. Simply put, if we are saved on the inside, we have a responsibility to live it on the outside! If we do, it will positively affect our attitudes toward others and will serve as a light in this dark world, leading them to the truth.

And now, He will spend a lengthy section of verses name-dropping in the very best of ways.

The like-mindedness of a Timothy

Philippians 2:19 *But I trust in the Lord Jesus to send Timotheus shortly unto you, that I also may be of good comfort, when I know your state.*

Paul ended the last section of verses with a reminder that the Philippians did not want to hear, a reminder that he may possibly be put to death. He made it clear that he was more than okay with that if it needed to be. So, as he begins this section, he turns to happier possibilities.

He begins by telling them that he trusts that he will be able to send Timothy to them very quickly so that he (Paul) can be comforted by having Timothy come back and tell him how the Philippians are doing. And the next verse explains why Paul would choose Timothy for that task.

Philippians 2:20 *For I have no man likeminded, who will naturally care for your state.*

This introduces us to our "on the one hand," our first of two men that Paul is going to write about. Paul said of Timothy, "I have no man likeminded." That word, likeminded, is a picturesque word. It is from *isosukon*, and it means "equal in soul." Paul was saying that Timothy had the same heart, soul, and thoughts toward the Philippians that he did. Timothy literally cared for the Philippians just as much as Paul did. And it was not a put-on; the word *naturally* means "sincerely,

70

genuinely." And this was important to Paul, especially in light of what he had to say in the very next verse.

Philippians 2:21 *For all seek their own, not the things which are Jesus Christ's.*

Other than Timothy, everyone else that Paul had with him (with one exception, as he will get to in a few verses) was about self rather than service. They all sought "their own": their own wants, needs, plans, and hopes, rather than the things of Christ. None of them were willing to make the trip to Philippi and care for others because their own things took priority over what Christ regarded as important.

In other letters of Paul, we will actually find some names attached to that problem. One of those names is Demas. Demas had once served alongside of Paul, but by the time Paul wrote 2 Timothy, he had this to say:

2 Timothy 4:10 *For Demas hath forsaken me, having loved this present world...*

Timothy, though, was different. Timothy had the same options as Demas: love the world or love the Lord. He chose to love the Lord, and that meant loving and serving others even when it was not convenient or profitable.

Philippians 2:22 *But ye know the proof of him, that, as a son with the father, he hath served with me in the gospel.*

In Acts 16 and 17, we read of Timothy serving there in Philippi alongside of Paul. So the Philippians knew him. They had first-hand proof that Timothy had been like a son to Paul as he served with him in the gospel. It seems that no one was ever quite as close as Timothy was to Paul.

Philippians 2:23 *Him therefore I hope to send presently, so soon as I shall see how it will go with me.*

The plan in this verse was pretty clear. Paul intended to send Timothy to the Philippians as soon as his trial was completed and he knew how things were going to go as far as him living, dying, remaining in captivity, or being set free.

The loyalty of an Epaphroditus

Philippians 2:24 *But I trust in the Lord that I also myself shall come shortly.* **25** *Yet I supposed it necessary to send to you Epaphroditus, my brother, and companion in labour, and fellowsoldier, but your messenger, and he that ministered to my wants.*

Paul intended to send Timothy to the Philippians. But he also very clearly planned on coming to them again himself. And from 1 Timothy 1:3, it seems that he actually did get to make that visit. But for the time being, with his fate uncertain, he intended to send another man to the Philippians, not just Timothy. In fact, he is going to go ahead and send that second man, Epaphroditus, carrying this letter. Epaphroditus is the exception to Paul's assertion that "all seek their own."

Look at how Paul was able to describe this dear man: *"my brother, and companion in labour, and fellowsoldier."* These are three pretty lofty terms when coming from a man like Paul!

When you see Paul call Epaphroditus a brother, regard it as bigger than simply being saved, a brother in Christ. Everyone already knew that, so that is not what Paul was saying. He meant it the same way we mean it when someone has become so close to us that we regard them as much more than a friend.

Companion in labor tells us that Epaphroditus was someone that Paul would dearly prize: an energetic worker for Christ. Anyone can get saved and go to heaven; some cannot stand to go to heaven without bringing others with them and spend their lives in that pursuit.

Fellowsoldier tells us that Epaphroditus understood the nature of the real Christian experience, unlike very many in his day and in ours. Here is how Paul put it to Timothy:

2 Timothy 2:3 *Thou therefore endure hardness, as a good **soldier** of Jesus Christ.* **4** *No man that warreth entangleth* *himself with the affairs of this life; that he may please him who hath chosen him to be a **soldier**.*

This is not a popular message. It is not an Osteenesque "Live your best life now" version of Christianity. But it is the Bible version of Christianity. We have an enemy, the devil, and we are at war.

This is quite possibly the biggest miss of modern Christianity. Modern Christianity has people boarding a proverbial cruise ship to glory. Bible Christianity has us boarding a battleship through troubled waters and preparing accordingly. And the more the modern church produces vacationers rather than soldiers, the weaker and more useless she will become.

All of this, brother, companion in labor, and fellowsoldier, is what Epaphroditus was to Paul. But to the Philippians, he was something else as well:

"but your messenger, and he that ministered to my wants."

Epaphroditus was one of the members of the church at Philippi. They chose him and sent him to Rome as their messenger to Paul. He is the one who ministered to Paul in their stead. And by "wants," Paul did not mean "luxuries or pleasures that I would really like." That word indicates a lack, a need to be met. Epaphroditus was the one who faithfully did that to Paul for the church at Philippi.

The next two verses give us another bit of insight into the character of this man, Epaphroditus.

Philippians 2:26 *For he longed after you all, and was full of heaviness, because that ye had heard that he had been sick. 27 For indeed he was sick nigh unto death: but God had mercy on him; and not on him only, but on me also, lest I should have sorrow upon sorrow.*

The fact that the Philippian church heard that Epaphroditus was sick lets us know that he was not sick when

73

they sent him. So either on the journey to Rome on their behalf, or at some point while he was there ministering to Paul, he got very sick, and somehow the Philippians found out about it.

Verse twenty-seven tells us that he very nearly died. And that makes verse twenty-six all the more remarkable. Epaphroditus' concern was not that he almost died but that the Philippians would be worried about him. He was brokenhearted to think that he may have caused them concern!

Yes, this part of his story had a happy ending. God had mercy on him by sparing his life. None of us are owed or guaranteed so much as another day, so every day that we live another day is the mercy of God! But Paul pointed out that God had mercy as much on him as on Epaphroditus by healing Epaphroditus. If you are in desperate need of a caregiver, you will be really grateful to God for every day that God keeps them healthy. If Epaphroditus had died, it would have given Paul what he called *"sorrow upon sorrow,"* meaning another sorrow to add to all the other sorrows that he already carried.

Philippians 2:28 *I sent him therefore the more carefully, that, when ye see him again, ye may rejoice, and that I may be the less sorrowful.*

When we see the word *carefully* in this verse, we may take it wrongly if we are not careful. While Paul was certainly going to be careful what he did with Epaphroditus or Timothy or any other fellow laborer, the carefulness that he speaks of in this verse was directed toward the Philippians, not toward Epaphroditus. The word is from the root *spouday,* and it means "with haste, with great dispatch." In other words, holding Epaphroditus back for a while longer for his own benefit would have been damaging to the Philippians who were so worried about him. So Paul carefully, with haste and great dispatch, sent Epaphroditus back to them. The purpose, according to the last half of the verse, was that *"when ye see him again, ye may rejoice, and that I may be the less sorrowful."* And this shows us that Paul had the same heart for the Philippians that Epaphroditus did; both of them were brokenhearted at the thought of them being worried.

Philippians 2:29 *Receive him therefore in the Lord with all gladness; and hold such in reputation:*

There is little question that the Philippians were going to do what Paul asked here anyway, especially the first part about receiving him in the Lord with all gladness. To receive him in the Lord meant to receive him as much more than just a human friend; no matter what position he held among them, even if it were that of the lowest servant, he had distinguished himself in the Lord's service and should be received with gladness as such.

That last phrase, *"hold such in reputation,"* means to highly honor and esteem him. In modern vernacular, it is much akin to what we say when we teach our young people to make heroes out of godly servants of the Lord rather than out of worldly stars. And why would anyone be worthy of such honor? Verse thirty answers that question clearly:

Philippians 2:30 *Because for the work of Christ he was nigh unto death, not regarding his life, to supply your lack of service toward me.*

That is an excellent definition of a real hero. Epaphroditus did not even think about his own life because of the great work of Christ he was doing, namely ministering to Paul in the place of the Philippians. He very nearly gave his life for the cause of Christ.

The man was faithful unto death and loyal to Paul.

From the outside looking in, it would seem that Paul did not have much. He had lost everything, repeatedly been beaten within an inch of his life, and was now in prison and possibly going to lose his life. But what he did have was a like-minded man named Timothy and a loyal man named Epaphroditus.

Anyone that has a couple of people like that is rich indeed.

Chapter Seven
Of Dogs and Doctrine

Philippians 3:1 *Finally, my brethren, rejoice in the Lord. To write the same things to you, to me indeed is not grievous, but for you it is safe. 2 Beware of dogs, beware of evil workers, beware of the concision. 3 For we are the circumcision, which worship God in the spirit, and rejoice in Christ Jesus, and have no confidence in the flesh. 4 Though I might also have confidence in the flesh. If any other man thinketh that he hath whereof he might trust in the flesh, I more: 5 Circumcised the eighth day, of the stock of Israel, of the tribe of Benjamin, an Hebrew of the Hebrews; as touching the law, a Pharisee; 6 Concerning zeal, persecuting the church; touching the righteousness which is in the law, blameless. 7 But what things were gain to me, those I counted loss for Christ. 8 Yea doubtless, and I count all things but loss for the excellency of the knowledge of Christ Jesus my Lord: for whom I have suffered the loss of all things, and do count them but dung, that I may win Christ, 9 And be found in him, not having mine own righteousness, which is of the law, but that which is through the faith of Christ, the righteousness which is of God by faith: 10 That I may know him, and the power of his resurrection, and the fellowship of his sufferings, being made conformable unto his death; 11 If by any means I might attain unto the resurrection of the dead.*

Paul used the last very long section of verses to get very personal with the Philippians, going on at length about how precious Timothy and Epaphroditus were to him. But now, as chapter three begins, the direction of content will shift drastically as Paul begins to deal with a pretty crucial doctrinal issue.

A word of rejoicing

Philippians 3:1 *Finally, my brethren, rejoice in the Lord. To write the same things to you, to me indeed is not grievous, but for you it is safe.*

From time to time, the different denominations will look back to the characters of Scripture and claim one great hero of the faith or another as one of their very own. But if we are to play that game, the battle for Paul will quickly be over.

Paul was a Baptist.

I say this with some confidence because, two chapters before he concluded his written message, he was already using the word "finally." And, to further buttress my assertion, look at Philippians 4:8.

Philippians 4:8 *Finally, brethren...*

So, halfway through his message, he was already claiming to be closing the message, and then he closed again with the same words one chapter later.

Obviously, I am teasing. But it is instructive to note that as Paul begins chapter 3, in his mind, he is already beginning to switch gears and to bring things to a close. And in this, his "first conclusion before the second conclusion," he begins with, *"Finally, my brethren, rejoice in the Lord."* This once again shows the nature and tone of the epistle to the Philippians. This was Paul's letter of joy to people that he dearly loved. And he wanted his beloved Philippians to be rejoicing in the Lord rather than to be mired down in the misery under which some that he will mention shortly would love to place them.

Never forget that the Christian life, properly understood and lived, is a rejoicing thing.

After giving this simple yet happy command, Paul uttered a cryptic-sounding warning, though, *"To write the same things to you, to me indeed is not grievous, but for you it is safe."*

When Paul spoke here of writing "the same things" to them, he was indicating that he had said these very things before and was going to get a bit repetitive. So what we will read in the following verses, along with what we read at the very beginning of verse one, was not new information to the Philippians; Paul had already told all of it to all of them previously. And that lets us know that it was pretty important since he is now restating it.

Paul said that writing these things again to them was not grievous to him. That means that it did not bother him to be going over these words again. Some things are important enough to be restated without apology or worry. And the content of this passage certainly was, as we see in Paul's words, *"but for you it is safe."* In other words, there was an issue of danger at hand, and them carefully heeding Paul's restated warning, beginning with the command to rejoice in the Lord, would lead them to a position of safety from the danger.

A warning of heresy

Philippians 3:2 *Beware of dogs, beware of evil workers, beware of the concision.*

There is not a single other verse in the entire Bible where there are multiple usages of the word *beware* in the same verse. But here, Paul uses it three times in just eleven words! And this clearly marks a stark change in the content and tone of this letter. Mind you, the entire letter is still about joy, but Paul is now switching gears to warn them about those who would completely rob all of that joy from them.

Paul mentions three things in this verse the Philippians were to beware of: dogs, evil workers, and the concision.

The first item on the list, dogs, was not talking about Chihuahuas and Labradoodles and Pit Bulls. It was a reference to two-legged dogs, people. Dogs in our day are normally calm and domesticated, simple pets. But in the first century, that was a rarity. Dogs were most commonly roving packs of mangy scavengers. So, for anyone to be referred to as a dog was not a compliment in the least. And as we will see from the content of the verses that follow, this was a reference to the Judaizers, the very same people that were causing so much trouble in Galatia.

The second item on the list, evil workers, is another way of designating the exact same group, the Judaizers. They proclaimed to be the arbiters of morality, but instead, they were producers of evil works.

The third item on the list, the concision, clearly lets us know that we are dealing with the Judaizers. The word for concision means cutting, and it was another way to describe circumcision, which Paul will mention in the very next verse.

Philippians 3:3 *For we are the circumcision, which worship God in the spirit, and rejoice in Christ Jesus, and have no confidence in the flesh.*

Judaizers had at some point made their way to Philippi and begun their work of trying to undermine the gospel of Jesus Christ that Paul had taught to the Philippians. As was the case almost everywhere he went, it was not just a matter of getting people to Christ but of then trying to keep them from being sucked into heresy that would rob them of their joy and vitality in Christ.

The Judaizers called themselves "the circumcision." But Paul said here to the Philippians the same thing that he said when he wrote to the church at Rome in different words, "we, we the saved, we are the real circumcision." And there are three litmus tests he laid out here to show the difference between the pseudo-circumcision of the Judaizers and the real circumcision of the believers in Christ.

Test number one was, *For we are the circumcision, which worship God in the spirit...*

These words are another indication that, contrary to what modern self-proclaimed Bible scholars teach, there was not one ounce of difference or one centimeter of space between the views of Christ and the views of Paul. Look at what Christ Himself said to the woman at the well that matches what Paul said here:

John 4:23 *But the hour cometh, and now is, when the true worshippers shall worship the Father **in spirit** and in truth: for the Father seeketh such to worship him.* **24** *God is a Spirit: and they that worship him must worship him **in spirit** and in truth.*

The Judaizers did not worship God in spirit; they "worshipped" Him in mechanical form and fashion. Their services were a liturgical checklist, not a living communication.

Test number two was, *"For we are the circumcision, which... rejoice in Christ Jesus."*

The Judaizers definitely did not rejoice in Christ Jesus. If they could have pushed a button and made His name and memory disappear from all of human history, every one of them would have done it without a second thought.

Test number three was, *"For we are the circumcision, which ...have no confidence in the flesh."*

The only confidence that the Judaizers did have was in the flesh. They could not possibly have cared less what was going on in your heart or soul or spirit; they just wanted to know if you had been circumcised.

What they believed and taught was heresy. And Paul's warnings concerning them as dogs and as evil workers and as the concision was "beware, beware, beware!"

When people are teaching heresy, we do not need to be welcoming; we need to beware.

A witness with credibility

Paul had just gotten done referring to the Judaizers as those who had confidence in the flesh. And in so doing, it seems that he knew that he was opening himself up to a potential attack that would go something like this:

"Paul is just saying that because nothing about him has ever been right; you need to listen to us instead because we have always been right in our flesh." Look how he immediately shifted to deal with that doubtless coming attack:

Philippians 3:4 *Though I might also have confidence in the flesh. If any other man thinketh that he hath whereof he might trust in the flesh, I more:*

Paul is now going to get into a brief battle of credentials with his adversaries, the Judaizers. They were going to do their best to paint him as an uncultured, uncouth, illiterate rube. This has forever been a favorite attack of the devil: discredit the messenger to discredit the message. But in Paul's case, that was not going to be an easy task; he claimed in verse four that if it were possible to have confidence in the flesh, then he would win that battle over all of his Judaizing adversaries because he had way more reason to be confident in the flesh than any of them.

What could possibly make him so bold as to make that claim? He will not take long to answer that question:

Philippians 3:5 *Circumcised the eighth day, of the stock of Israel, of the tribe of Benjamin, an Hebrew of the Hebrews; as touching the law, a Pharisee;* **6** *Concerning zeal, persecuting the church; touching the righteousness which is in the law, blameless.*

Paul, in these verses, lays out seven layers of qualifications that he possessed, making up a package that few, if any, could have ever matched.

His first credential was that he was circumcised on the eighth day. This was exactly to the day what the law required:

Leviticus 12:3 *And in the eighth day the flesh of his foreskin shall be circumcised.*

Albert Barnes observed that "it is probable that, in some cases, this was delayed on account of sickness, or from some other cause; and, in the case of proselytes, it was not performed until adult age." (Linder) But with Paul, there was no delay. Among the Judaizers, there were almost certainly a great many who had been circumcised, but not on that exact day. Paul, though, had.

His second credential was that he was *"of the stock of Israel."* Once again, let me give you Albert Barnes on this. He says of it that Paul was:

"Descended from the patriarch Israel, or Jacob; and, therefore, able to trace his genealogy back as far as any Jew could. He was not a proselyte himself from among the heathen, nor were any of his ancestors proselytes. He had all the advantages which could be derived from a regular descent from the venerable founders of the Jewish nation. He was thus distinguished from the Edomites and others who practised circumcision; from the Samaritans, who were made up of a mixture of people; and from many, even among the Jews, whose ancestors had been once heathen, and who had become proselytes." (Linder)

So, Paul was an Israelite all the way back, and there was nothing else but that in his background. Not many of the Judaizers could say that, but he could.

His third credential was that he was *"of the tribe of Benjamin."* So Paul was not just a Jew; he was of a very important tribe out of the twelve. Benjamin was both the tribe in which the monarchy began under Saul and, along with Judah, one of the two tribes that did not revolt along with the other ten when the kingdom split. Again, there were a great many of the Judaizers who could not say that, but Paul could.

His fourth credential was that he was "*an Hebrew of the Hebrews*," and this was very important in the days of Hellenism. A lot of the Jews grew up with the Greek language and the Greek mindset and the Greek culture as their primary identity. But a minority of the Jews continued to maintain the Hebrew language as their primary language, the Hebrew mindset as their primary way of thinking, and Hebrew culture as their way of living. Paul was one of those minorities that did so.

His fifth credential was "*as touching the law, a Pharisee.*" This meant that as far as the law went, he was part of the group that held the strictest interpretation of it, as opposed to the more liberal Sadducees. Not all of the Judaizers could say that, but Paul could.

His sixth credential was "*Concerning zeal, persecuting the church.*" Some among the Judaizers had merely scoffed at the church; Paul had actively tried to stamp it out. And if it, the church, were in error, then Paul was far more right in how he formerly treated the church than the Judaizers who merely made fun of it and mocked it.

So again, Paul could say that he had such zeal that he had once persecuted the church. Not all of the Judaizers could say that, but Paul could.

His seventh credential is found in these concluding words, "*touching the righteousness which is in the law, blameless.*"

That is a breathtaking statement. It means that from the time of his youth up, Paul had scrupulously kept the law to such a degree that he would be regarded as blameless. Mind you, no one ever kept the law perfectly other than Christ, but Paul kept it to such a degree that among humans, there was literally no one better, and no one was ever willing to point a finger of blame at him.

The Judaizers could not say this; Paul could. So when they came around and tried to paint him as an unqualified, uncouth, illiterate rube, it simply was not going to work!

A winning that matters

Philippians 3:7 *But what things were gain to me, those I counted loss for Christ.*

The little conjunction *but* that begins this verse is once again from the strong adversative, *alla*. In other words, this is not a slight shift that Paul is about to introduce; it is a whiplash. He has just gotten done describing all of the things in his past that the world would look to and glorify him in, and now he is whipping the theological vehicle into a 180 and leaving tire tracks smoking in the exact opposite direction. All of those things that the Judaizers especially would regard as being so impressive, those things that Paul here described as once being "gain to him," he now counted those things as loss for Christ.

Gain, in this verse, means profit, profitable, advantageous.

Loss in this verse means the exact opposite: damage, disadvantage, forfeit. They stand in stark contrast the one to the other. All of the things that Paul once regarded as treasures he now views as trash in comparison to what he now has in Christ. But as shocking as that is, he is not even going to stop there.

Philippians 3:8 *Yea doubtless, and I count all things but loss for the excellency of the knowledge of Christ Jesus my Lord: for whom I have suffered the loss of all things, and do count them but dung, that I may win Christ,* **9** *And be found in him, not having mine own righteousness, which is of the law, but that which is through the faith of Christ, the righteousness which is of God by faith:* **10** *That I may know him, and the power of his resurrection, and the fellowship of his sufferings, being made conformable unto his death;* **11** *If by any means I might attain unto the resurrection of the dead.*

These four verses make up one long sentence, one continuous thought.

He began by saying, *"Yea doubtless, and I count all things but loss for the excellency of the knowledge of Christ Jesus my Lord:"*

In our terms, Paul just said something akin to, "Without a single doubt, I regard absolutely everything as loss for the excellency of the knowledge of Christ Jesus my Lord." So Paul was not just looking back to his seven qualifications and regarding them as a worthwhile loss. He regarded everything as a worthwhile loss if it would lead to the most excellent and superior knowledge available to mankind, the knowledge of Christ Jesus, whom he rightly regarded as his Lord.

This was not just a philosophical statement to Paul. Look at how he ended verse eight:

...for whom I have suffered the loss of all things, and do count them but dung, that I may win Christ,

What does Paul mean when he speaks of having suffered the loss of all things? He means that "in accepting Christ he gave up all that the world holds dear." (Linder, People's New Testament Commentary)

Friends, family, future prospects, comfort, name the category, and Paul willingly suffered loss in that category when he chose to follow Christ. But far from looking back on those things and lamenting the treasures that he had lost, he chose to regard them as dung, manure.

Does this indicate hatred and disgust on Paul's part for family or friends? Certainly not. He wrote often and at length of his love for his people. But it means that when looked upon it in the sense of value, Paul understood that what he gained in Christ was of so much more value than what he gave up that he could regard all of his loss as dung so that he could "win Christ." And this is not said in the sense of salvation alone but also in the sense of gaining so much of Christ in his day-to-day life that he would

86

become Christlike himself. Look at how verse nine continues that thought:

And be found in him, not having mine own righteousness, which is of the law, but that which is through the faith of Christ, the righteousness which is of God by faith:

Once again, though this does include salvation, it does not stop with salvation. By any and all who would investigate, be it God or man, Paul wanted to be found in Christ. And what follows, "*not having mine own righteousness, which is of the law, but that which is through the faith of Christ, the righteousness which is of God by faith,*" takes us right back to the contrast between himself and the Judaizers. They had their own "righteousness," the keeping of the law to the best of their ability. Paul once had the same and an even greater measure.

But he no longer wanted that. He wanted the righteousness which comes through the *faith of Christ, the righteousness which is of God by faith.* He knew that the righteousness that he once had was imperfect and could not save and could not please God on a day-by-day basis. So by strong contrast once again, he now wanted the righteousness that was perfect and could save and did please God on a day-by-day basis, the righteousness that only comes from believing, placing one's absolute faith in the Lord Jesus Christ.

That was so different than anything he had ever had before. Previously, it had all been about how good he could be in his own efforts and under his own power. But once he finally realized how useless that was, he was able to start leaning on that which was not useless. And all of that had a purpose, a purpose that goes far beyond just escaping hell. Here is how he continued the thought in verse ten:

That I may know him, and the power of his resurrection, and the fellowship of his sufferings, being made conformable unto his death;

Paul was clearly a saved man, so his desire here to *"know him"* had nothing to do with being born again all over. He was indicating that he wanted to have a personal, experiential knowledge of Christ. He wanted to be close to Him. He wanted to know what his precious Christ likes and does not like, wants and does not want; he wanted to be spiritually intimate with his Lord. And this, truly knowing Christ, ought to be the heart cry and passionate pursuit of every single true believer until we stand in His presence and see Him face-to-face.

In this, Paul also wanted to know *the power of his resurrection.* This is talking about the day-by-day power of the resurrection in our lives. Simply put, the resurrection of Christ did not just grant victory over death; it also provided for us victory in our lives. Since we serve a living Savior, His resurrection empowers us as we live for Him.

From that lovely pinnacle of power, though, Paul ends verse ten with what some would mistakenly regard as a decidedly darker thought, *"and the fellowship of his sufferings, being made conformable unto his death."*

Everyone wants the power; few want the pain. But fellowship with Christ is a fellowship of suffering. He suffered for us and allows us the privilege to suffer for Him. And it is in that suffering *for* Christ that we will be drawn nearer *to* Christ than by any other means. And for Paul, he wanted it to go so far as *"being made conformable unto his death."* Paul looked at the possibility of being a martyr for Christ, and, far from shrinking from it, he recognized it as the final and highest honor possible in a human life.

Paul closes out this section of thought with the unique words of verse eleven:

If by any means I might attain unto the resurrection of the dead.

At first blush, it sounds as if Paul is looking for a way to earn salvation. We know, obviously, that is not the case. By this

88

point, Paul has already written extensively about salvation being by grace through faith in Christ, including just a short few verses ago. So when he speaks here of attaining unto the resurrection of the dead, and when he uses the introductory phrase "if by any means," he is looking at the resurrection in a very different light at this point.

Here is that different light, as seen from another passage from the pen of Paul:

Colossians 3:1 *If ye then be risen with Christ, seek those things which are above, where Christ sitteth on the right hand of God.*

Paul spoke to the believers in Colosse about being risen with Christ as something that had already happened, not as something they were looking forward to. And he did so in the context of changed desires and a changed life.

What Paul was saying both to the church at Philippi and the church at Colosse was that though we were guaranteed a future resurrection of our bodies upon the moment we got saved, we were also presented with the possibility of present resurrection even now, a resurrection to an earthly life lived fully for Christ. We once were dead in trespasses and sins but have now been made alive in Christ (Ephesians 2:1), and are to be "*by any means*" earning that distinction in our daily lives.

We could put it this way: Paul did not just want to go to heaven after he left Earth; he wanted to truly live like a citizen of heaven every day that he lived on Earth.

Chapter Eight
Apprehended

Philippians 3:12 *Not as though I had already attained, either were already perfect: but I follow after, if that I may apprehend that for which also I am apprehended of Christ Jesus.* **13** *Brethren, I count not myself to have apprehended: but this one thing I do, forgetting those things which are behind, and reaching forth unto those things which are before,* **14** *I press toward the mark for the prize of the high calling of God in Christ Jesus.* **15** *Let us therefore, as many as be perfect, be thus minded: and if in any thing ye be otherwise minded, God shall reveal even this unto you.* **16** *Nevertheless, whereto we have already attained, let us walk by the same rule, let us mind the same thing.* **17** *Brethren, be followers together of me, and mark them which walk so as ye have us for an ensample.* **18** *(For many walk, of whom I have told you often, and now tell you even weeping, that they are the enemies of the cross of Christ:* **19** *Whose end is destruction, whose God is their belly, and whose glory is in their shame, who mind earthly things.)* **20** *For our conversation is in heaven; from whence also we look for the Saviour, the Lord Jesus Christ:* **21** *Who shall change our vile body, that it may be fashioned like unto his glorious body, according to the working whereby he is able even to subdue all things unto himself.*

Paul got very doctrinal in the last section of verses. And yet, while many "theologians" get very proud, some even to the point of absolute arrogance, Paul did not. And the section of verses we are now examining is an excellent demonstration of that fact.

A lack of arrival

Philippians 3:12 *Not as though I had already attained, either were already perfect: but I follow after, if that I may apprehend that for which also I am apprehended of Christ Jesus.* **13a** *Brethren, I count not myself to have apprehended...*

Paul spent verses four through six giving his previous credentials as a lost religious man:

Philippians 3:4 *Though I might also have confidence in the flesh. If any other man thinketh that he hath whereof he might trust in the flesh, I more:* **5** *Circumcised the eighth day, of the stock of Israel, of the tribe of Benjamin, an Hebrew of the Hebrews; as touching the law, a Pharisee;* **6** *Concerning zeal, persecuting the church; touching the righteousness which is in the law, blameless.*

Then he spent verses seven through ten giving his new credentials as a saved man:

Philippians 3:7 *But what things were gain to me, those I counted loss for Christ.* **8** *Yea doubtless, and I count all things but loss for the excellency of the knowledge of Christ Jesus my Lord: for whom I have suffered the loss of all things, and do count them but dung, that I may win Christ,* **9** *And be found in him, not having mine own righteousness, which is of the law, but that which is through the faith of Christ, the righteousness which is of God by faith:* **10** *That I may know him, and the power of his resurrection, and the fellowship of his sufferings, being made conformable unto his death;*

Those are glowing words and glorious credentials. And yet, at that point, the humility of Paul kicked in. He clearly did not want to be seen as a Christian braggart. And that is why he follows all of that up in verse twelve with:

"Not as though I had already attained, either were already perfect:"

These words simply mean, "I have not arrived yet; I still have a lot of growing to do in the spiritual life."

This is Paul we are talking about, the man who wrote at least thirteen books of the New Testament, went on three huge missionary journeys, started countless churches, won multitudes to Christ, and suffered every step of the way in so doing. If he had not arrived, WE have not arrived!

Paul then writes, *"but I follow after..."* That means "I am pursuing it." He is saying, "This perfection in my spiritual walk that I wish I had, I am not simply sitting back wishing for it; I am actively pursuing it every single moment of every single day." And far from being a personal goal that would displease Christ, the next thing we read is, *"if that I may apprehend that for which also I am apprehended of Christ Jesus."*

You surely have noticed that double reference to apprehend or apprehended, and you have likely also noticed that it is found in the very next verse as well. And in all three cases, it is from the word *katalambano,* and means "to lay hold on something and make it yours." And notice the two different directions that comes from. Again, Paul said, *"if that **I may apprehend** that for which also **I am apprehended** of Christ Jesus."*

I may apprehend; I am apprehended. When you see those different directional phrases in the light of the definition "to lay hold on something and make it yours," you realize that Paul is saying something like, "I am pursuing; I am expending the greatest possible efforts to lay hold on the thing that Christ laid hold on me for."

Scripture itself is very clear on what exactly it is that Christ laid hold on us for:

Romans 8:29 *For whom he did foreknow, he also did predestinate* **to be conformed to the image of his Son**, *that he might be the firstborn among many brethren.*

Christ does not lay hold on people just to save them from the fire; He lays hold on people to fulfill the Father's purpose of seeing them conformed into His image here and now. We call this Christlikeness. Paul's daily goal was to be Christlike because that was Christ's goal for Paul. And it is His goal for all of us as well and, therefore, should be our goal as well. Our days should not be consumed with thoughts of being comfortable; our days should be consumed with thoughts of being Christlike. This is what we ought to be striving to apprehend, to lay hold on and make it ours, because that is why Christ laid hold on us and made us His.

And yet, look at what this greatest of all Christians said at the very beginning of the next verse:

Philippians 3:13a *Brethren, I count not myself to have apprehended...*

Was Paul striving with all his might to be Christlike? Yes. Was he satisfied that he had accomplished that goal? No, not at all. When Paul looked at himself each morning, he always saw the need for greater Christlikeness on that new day than he had on the day before. The day that you and I believe we have arrived at perfect Christlikeness is likely the day that we are farther away than we have ever been.

A looking ahead

Philippians 3:13b *...but this one thing I do, forgetting those things which are behind, and reaching forth unto those things which are before,* **14** *I press toward the mark for the prize of the high calling of God in Christ Jesus.*

For any Christian struggling with either the past or with pride, there are no greater words of instruction in the entire Bible than what you find in these verses. Paul begins by saying, *"But this one thing I do."*

The fact that he is going to give a one-item list is really helpful; the more items on the list, the more likely we are to forget something. Paul said, "But this one thing I do," and then he spelled it out for us. And as he does, we see that it is one thing made up of two directions.

Direction number one is *"forgetting those things which are **behind**."* And please take note that this is not an accidental forgetting; this is volitional, not accidental. Paul is choosing to forget, choosing not to remember.

And what exactly were those things in the past?

They were all of the negatives from verses five and six, but they were also all of the positives from seven through eleven! You see, whether you are anchored in the negatives of the past or anchored in the positives of the past, you are still anchored in the past! When you try to leave the parking lot, whether your car is chained to ten tons of garbage or ten tons of gold, it still isn't going anywhere.

Paul's entire point is that each new day that we awake, we have to put the past behind us and lay hold on the pursuit of greater Christlikeness for that day.

There are a lot of truly saved individuals who never really do become Christlike because they never really do let go of their past. So direction number one is "forgetting those things which are **behind**."

But direction number two is *"reaching forth unto those things which are **before**,"* meaning ahead, out in front of you. And verse fourteen tells us what those things are, saying, *"I press toward the mark for the prize of the high calling of God in Christ Jesus."*

To press toward means to run hard towards. It is the picture of someone who has the finish line in sight and will not let adversaries or competitors or exhaustion or discouragement keep them from running the next step and the next step and the next step until they cross the finish line. And the finish line, in this case, is the mark, meaning the goal, *"for the prize of the high calling of God in Christ Jesus."*

Once again, that high calling is Christlikeness in our lives. And it both is a prize and brings us prizes from God, rewards for our efforts.

There is no greater calling and no greater goal in any Christian's life than being like Christ. And we will never, ever do that while focused on the past. The past has got to be let go in favor of the present pursuit of crossing the finish line in the daily race to be like Him.

Philippians 3:15 *Let us therefore, as many as be perfect, be thus minded: and if in any thing ye be otherwise minded, God shall reveal even this unto you.*

If you are the observant sort, you know that as we enter verse fifteen, we have a bit of a mystery to clear up. In verse twelve, Paul very plainly said that he was not perfect, and yet here, in verse fifteen, it sounds like he is including himself among those who are perfect. What exactly is going on with that? The answer to your question can be found in another question, the question "in what?"

I have never a single moment in my life been perfect at being the fastest runner on the planet. But I have been perfect at completely running a 5K from start to finish, not leaving off a single step.

In verse twelve, Paul was talking about perfection in Christlikeness; in verse fifteen, Paul was talking about perfection in pursuing Christlikeness. The word in both cases is from the same root word, *telos,* and it means "completion, lacking nothing." Applied to what we are looking at here, Paul was saying, "I do lack when it comes to Christlikeness, but I lack nothing when it comes to the pursuit of Christlikeness." And that is what Paul was encouraging among the Philippian believers when he said, "*Let us therefore, as many as be perfect, be thus minded.*" In other words, let's all think the same way on this. And he then ended with the warning "*and if in any thing ye be otherwise minded, God shall reveal even this unto you.*"

He was telling them that if there was an area in their life in which they were not minded to pursue Christlikeness, God would reveal it to them. Paul was convinced that they were saved and, therefore, that the Holy Ghost of God would be working in their heart every single day to accomplish the specific purpose that he had for them, namely present-day Christlikeness. And this, by the way, is a very good reason not to spend all of our time focusing on what other believers are or are not doing right as far as we are concerned. While different Scriptures instruct us in some circumstances to admonish or even rebuke one another, commands that we absolutely should obey when necessary, the Holy Ghost is very good at His job, and we do not need to spend our time trying to do it for Him.

A "let us" attained

Philippians 3:16 *Nevertheless, whereto we have already attained, let us walk by the same rule, let us mind the same thing.*

Let me paraphrase this for you to give you a good sense of it. "Nevertheless, even though we just covered all of that, to whatever different degree different ones of us have been successful in this pursuit, let's all walk by the same rule [the same measuring rod], and mind the same thing, let's just all keep pressing on toward that mark."

Here is why that phrase was so important to the Philippians then and us now. All of them were at different stages of their Christian walk, and all of us are at different stages of our Christian walk. Whether we are ahead of or behind someone else in the pursuit of Christlikeness or whether someone else is ahead of or behind us in the pursuit of Christlikeness is not the main point. The main point is that we are all to start from wherever

97

we are each day and pursue it by God's measurements, heading for the same finish line.

If we do it this way, we will neither be discouraged by others who are farther advanced than we are nor will we be disgusted by those who are less advanced than we are. We will simply love each other and cheer each other on and follow after those who are ahead of us and encourage those who are behind us. The point in this particular race is to get everybody across the exact same finish line, Christlikeness, mostly by making sure that we are doing it rather than casting our eyes on everyone else in some negative way.

A leading arrangement

Philippians 3:17 *Brethren, be followers together of me, and mark them which walk so as ye have us for an ensample.*

Paul has been painting the picture of running the Christian race with the finish line being absolute Christlikeness. And in that picture and in that context, he then tells the Philippians in so many words, "Be followers together of me and also pay close attention to others who also walk like I walk, and follow them as well. Let us be your ensamples, your patterns of behavior."

It is a beautiful thing to realize that Paul was able to safely tell the Philippians to follow him and others who served alongside him. We so often hear people make the pseudo-pious statement, "Don't follow me, follow Christ." But that is an absolute copout. Those who have been saved longer than others ought to live their lives in such a way that they can turn around to those who are baby Christians and say, "If you haven't got it all figured out yet, just follow me; I will show you the way." And if we can't, we ought to fix the problem so that we can.

And in the case of the Philippian church, there were definitely some who had the problem of not being able to be followed. In fact, there were some that would be an utter disaster for anyone in Philippi to follow:

Philippians 3:18 *(For many walk, of whom I have told you often, and now tell you even weeping, that they are the enemies of the cross of Christ:* **19** *Whose end is destruction, whose God is their belly, and whose glory is in their shame, who mind earthly things.)*

Paul was not speaking metaphorically when he wrote these words. There were tears spattering the parchment as he wrote to tell them once again of what he had told them many times before. There were some people who, rather than being allies of the cross, were enemies of the cross. And the cross is put here for a euphemism of the gospel itself.

These people were not heading for heaven; verse nineteen tells us that their end is destruction. They very likely claimed to be saved, but they were utterly lost, the enemies of Christ, and heading for hell. You see, they had God; they just had the wrong one. Their God was their belly, according to verse nineteen. And this means that their desires were their deities. Whatever their flesh wanted, their flesh got. They bowed at the altar of pleasure and worshipped in the church of self. Their glory was not in Christ or the cross; their glory was in their shame. Albert Barnes rightly said of this, "That is, they glory in things of which they ought to be ashamed. They indulge in modes of living which ought to cover them with confusion." (Linder)

Paul closed verse nineteen by describing them as people *"who mind earthly things."* Their affections were not set on that which is above; their affections were firmly set on that which is below. No wonder Paul was so adamant that his dear believers in Philippi follow him and those who walked like him rather than these flamboyant, fleshly, fetid fakers.

Be very careful who you follow. If you follow the wrong people, you end up at the wrong destination. If you follow those who are godly, you will arrive at Christlikeness; if you follow those who are godless, you will arrive at carnality.

And why exactly was Paul so adamant about this? Verse twenty answers that question:

Philippians 3:20 *For our conversation is in heaven; from whence also we look for the Saviour, the Lord Jesus Christ:*

The word "conversation" in this verse is from the word *politeuma,* and it means "citizenship." When we think in our day of conversation, we think just of talking. When they thought of conversation, they thought of an entire identity and an entire way of living. As citizens of heaven, everything about us is to be different. As citizens of heaven, we are to be looking for the return of our Savior, the Lord Jesus Christ. And if we are, we will not follow those who lead us to be less Christlike; we will only follow those who lead us to be more Christlike since today may be the very day that we see Christ face-to-face.

A life awaiting

Philippians 3:21 *Who shall change our vile body, that it may be fashioned like unto his glorious body, according to the working whereby he is able even to subdue all things unto himself.*

The Who in verse twenty-one refers back to Christ our Lord and Savior from verse twenty. Paul just finished reminding us that we are looking for Him to come back from heaven. And now he tells us that when He does, He will *"change our vile body, that it may be fashioned like unto his glorious body."*

Here is how he put that thought to the church at Corinth:

1 Corinthians 15:51 *Behold, I shew you a mystery; We shall not all sleep, but we shall all be changed,* **52** *In a moment, in the twinkling of an eye, at the last trump: for the trumpet shall sound, and the dead shall be raised **incorruptible**, and we shall be **changed**.* **53** *For this corruptible must put on incorruption, and this mortal must put on immortality.*

Every day of our lives, even as we pursue present-day Christlikeness, we are corruptible. We can get it right for a day or a week or a month or a year or a decade and then stumble and fall flat on our spiritual faces the very next day. But when Christ comes, He will change our vile bodies and make them like His glorious body. And he is speaking in terms of righteousness. In other words, we are striving for Christlikeness all the while our flesh is desiring and demanding sin. But when He remakes our bodies, our flesh will no longer even desire or demand sin any longer. It will no longer interest us since it does not interest Him.

And just in case any of the believers in Philippi would wonder whether He could really do that, whether He really had that kind of power, Paul closed out this section of thought by saying, *"according to the working whereby he is able even to subdue all things unto himself."*

I absolutely love the way Adam Clarke explains this phrase:

> "Thus we find that the resurrection of the body is attributed to that power which governs and subdues all things, for nothing less than the energy that produced the human body at the beginning, can restore it from its lapsed and degraded state into that state of glory which it had at its creation, and render it capable of enjoying God throughout eternity." (504)

God wants us to pursue Christlikeness all day, every day, even now in these fleshly bodies. But we will never quite "apprehend" that goal perfectly. But when He comes, we will finally and fully be apprehended for that purpose.

Chapter Nine
From People Problems to Peace

Philippians 4:1 *Therefore, my brethren dearly beloved and longed for, my joy and crown, so stand fast in the Lord, my dearly beloved.* **2** *I beseech Euodias, and beseech Syntyche, that they be of the same mind in the Lord.* **3** *And I intreat thee also, true yokefellow, help those women which laboured with me in the gospel, with Clement also, and with other my fellowlabourers, whose names are in the book of life.* **4** *Rejoice in the Lord alway: and again I say, Rejoice.* **5** *Let your moderation be known unto all men. The Lord is at hand.* **6** *Be careful for nothing; but in every thing by prayer and supplication with thanksgiving let your requests be made known unto God.* **7** *And the peace of God, which passeth all understanding, shall keep your hearts and minds through Christ Jesus.*

Paul now brings us into the last chapter of this joyful letter. He just finished telling the believers in Philippi that they were going to be ushered into His presence one day and forever changed even in their bodies. But now, as he starts to wrap things up, he will take a few verses to come down to the present reality, which was not always quite as glorious.

103

Stand fast

Philippians 4:1 *Therefore, my brethren dearly beloved and longed for, my joy and crown, so stand fast in the Lord, my dearly beloved.*

The therefore that begins chapter four refers back to what was said in the last two verses of chapter three, namely that we are citizens of heaven and that Jesus is coming again. On that basis, Paul wrote to these Philippian believers, whom he called brethren, dearly beloved and longed for, and his joy and crown, and told them to stand fast in the Lord, closing out the verse by calling them dearly beloved yet again.

If you get the sense Paul really loved these people in Philippi, it is because he did.

By calling them dearly beloved twice, he was telling them that he had the deepest kind of love for them, the very *agapay* love of Christ.

By telling them that they were longed for, he was expressing a desire for them. He would have liked nothing better than to be with them where they were or have them with him where he was.

When he called them my joy and crown, he was telling them that he took delight in them and that they were like the crown on someone's head that would be their most prized possession.

And Paul's command to these people whom he loved so dearly was that they stand fast in Christ. He knew that everywhere they turned, there were adversaries who wanted to turn them away from Christ. So he was telling them to lock in place and dig deep roots and never budge even an inch in their relationship with Christ and in the doctrine He had imparted to them.

Shut down the cat fight

Philippians 4:2 *I beseech Euodias, and beseech Syntyche, that they be of the same mind in the Lord.*

We now arrive at a very personal and prickly point in the epistle. In this verse, we find two ladies, Euodias and Syntyche, and the reference to them is not a good one. They were not of the same mind in the Lord, which means, in simple terms, that they were fighting and feuding.

How heartbreaking and how stressful did it have to be to Paul to deal with something like this in his bonds? How heartbreaking and stressful did it have to be to whomever the pastor was there in Philippi? This was such a good church, and the personal conflict between two ladies had reached such a pitched crescendo that Paul literally had to write a letter about it and call them by name.

The way he did it, though, shows an amazing tactfulness in the midst of rebuke. Notice that he very carefully uses the word beseech of both ladies. A simpler way to write that sentence would be "I beseech Euodias and Syntyche" or "I beseech Syntyche and Euodias." But if he had done so, whoever was mentioned first would have probably taken offense because the second one would seem like an add-on.

I admire Paul's wisdom in that, but it also makes me cringe just a bit. He is having to very carefully parse every word of every phrase to make sure his words cannot be used to make things worse. He is, in so many words, having to walk on eggshells around these two ladies. Whether man or woman, when people in a church begin to fight and fuss and feud, God's man will get ulcers, and people around the combatants will get a strong desire to go elsewhere. If you really love the church and want to see it blessed, get along. It isn't really hard; after all, we teach that to our children from their earliest days.

Do not ever become a Euodias and Syntyche, or as I heard a radio preacher describe them many years ago, "You're Odious and Soon Touchy."

Support the servants

Philippians 4:3 *And I intreat thee also, true yokefellow, help those women which laboured with me in the gospel, with Clement also, and with other my fellowlabourers, whose names are in the book of life.*

As we get into verse three, you should know that there are a couple of mysteries within it. Paul has just gotten done asking Euodias and Syntyche to get along. And he goes straight from there into intreating, which means something like begging, a true yokefellow to help those women which labored with him in the gospel.

Mystery number one is who this true yokefellow is. We know that it is a singular individual, and we know that it is a man; the grammar is very clear on that. What we do not know is whether or not true yokefellow is a descriptive phrase of someone that Paul, for some reason, did not want to name or if it is actually the name itself. *Sudzuge,* the word that yoke fellow comes from, can either be a name or title.

Whoever this was, Paul clearly had a lot of confidence in him, as we can see by him calling him a *true* yokefellow. True is from *gnayseos*, and it means "genuine." Whoever this man was, he was genuine and a genuine help to Paul.

Mystery number two is who the ladies were that Paul mentions as having labored with him in the gospel. Some excellent men and commentators view this as a reference to Euodias and Syntyche themselves, and as a request that the true yoke fellow help them to get reconciled. For what it is worth, I cannot bring myself to go along with that position. Just the simple wording of the text very much seems to me to indicate that Paul is talking about a different group of women who had labored with him in the gospel and asking this true yokefellow to help them.

The word he uses for help is a strong word, *sullambanou*, and it means "to take hold of." In other words, whoever these ladies are, Paul was not just asking this yokefellow to pray for them now and then; he was asking him to really get into the trenches and give them substantial help. And as a good motivation for doing so, he went on to point out that these ladies had not only served with Paul but also with a man named Clement and with all their fellow laborers, all of whom had their names written in the Book of Life.

This entire verse, while it presents many mysteries as to identity, presents something very clear about influence. There were some ladies who had made a difference in the lives of those who were making a difference. The power of godly ladies in a church is unfathomable. When the ladies in the church are right, it is like a strong and pleasant breeze in the sails of a minister and a ministry. And, to complete the circle, please remember that Paul was asking a man to help the ladies who were helping the men. The early church was not a situation of segregation in which the ladies played no role. They were so helpful to the pastors and apostles that the apostle Paul told a man, "Help those ladies!"

Shout the victory

Philippians 4:4 *Rejoice in the Lord alway: and again I say, Rejoice.*

This almost seems like the oddest of segues in the text. Paul has written to admonish these two feuding females to get right with each other, and he has asked a man in whom he had much confidence to support some other ladies who had been such a help to him and others. And then, he seems to flip the switch away from pointed personal matters back to the original joyful tone of the letter. He addresses all of the believers in

Philippi, tells them to rejoice in the Lord alway, which we in our day would add an "S" to the end of, and then repeats that command to rejoice.

Yes, Paul had to deal with a very personal and prickly issue. But he had enough sense to deal with it and drop it rather than beating a dead horse into the ground. He told them what to do and then backed off and gave them room to do it. And then he immediately turned their attention back to rejoicing in the Lord.

There is nothing so infectious as rejoicing. And as Christians, we have more reason to rejoice than anyone else!

Show moderation

Philippians 4:5 *Let your moderation be known unto all men. The Lord is at hand.*

We should begin in this verse by defining the keyword, namely moderation. It is from the word *epieikays*, and it means "that which is seemly, suitable, equitable, mild, gentle, patient, and fair." It indicates a manner of life in which we both behave appropriately as an individual in everything and treat each other kindly and patiently. Clearly, then, there is a mouthful just in that one word.

On the first aspect of it, far too few Christians anymore behave appropriately as an individual in everything. We behave like the world, talk like the world, dress like the world, take in the entertainment of the world, and absorb the values of the world. There is little in modern Christianity that stands out anymore as being different from the world around it. And that is direct rebellion against the command of this verse.

On the second aspect of it, far too few Christians anymore treat each other kindly and patiently, let alone treat those in the world kindly and patiently. The way we behave toward our brothers and sisters in Christ, and toward our families, and toward our neighbors, and toward waiters and waitresses, and toward police officers, and toward all the random people that we meet all throughout our day, is generally far more unkind and impatient than kind and patient. And that, also, is direct rebellion against the command of this verse.

It is interesting to notice how Paul phrased this verse when he wrote it. As always, the translators did a perfect job smoothing it out for us. And that is good because the way Paul wrote it was something like *the moderation of you, make it known to all men.* That moderation was being heavily emphasized, and Paul was demanding, not asking, that they make it known to everyone. This verse gives a concrete expectation that we do right personally and to others and that we be open and vocal about it. In other words, Paul was not looking for closet Christians here; he was trying to produce people who would shine as lights in the world. And the impetus for the command in this verse was, *"The Lord is at hand."* Paul knew that the Lord can return at any time and that we, therefore, must absolutely always be ready. There can be no greater tragedy than Christ coming back right in the midst of us treating someone badly or in the midst of us demonstrating a very poor testimony to the world.

Stop worrying

Philippians 4:6 *Be careful for nothing; but in every thing by prayer and supplication with thanksgiving let your requests be made known unto God.* **7** *And the peace of God, which passeth all understanding, shall keep your hearts and minds through Christ Jesus.*

These are some of the most beautiful and beloved verses in the entire Bible and for very good reason. Paul begins by saying, *Be careful for nothing.* And he does not mean that they are not to be careful in the sense of being properly cautious; he means full of care, full of worry. And the way he said it lets us know that the Philippians had already gone that way; they were

109

already worrying and fretting and fuming and wringing their hands about the future. Paul told them to stop; he told them to literally not be full of care for anything whatsoever.

When we think of the things we face in our lives or could potentially face our lives, we immediately come to countless situations in our mind that we would no doubt be worried to death over should they take place. So, how, then, are we to arrive at being careful for nothing?

As you may suspect by this point in our study, the answer begins with a strong adversative, that little conjunction "but," that is once again from *alla*. Paul says, "*Be careful for nothing, but* [by strong contrast], *in every thing by prayer and supplication with thanksgiving let your requests be made known unto God.*"

Notice the juxtaposition of nothing and everything. If we are ever going to arrive at a state where we are careful for *nothing*, then we must pray about *everything*.

What exactly is prayer and supplication with thanksgiving? Prayer simply means it as we think of the word, praying, talking to God. Supplication is a tad bit more specific, meaning "to present our entreaties, to tell God about our needs." So we are to pray in general, we are to present our needs in specific, and then we are to spend time in that very same prayer in giving of thanks. This is the methodology by which we are to present our requests unto God.

And what will be the result of praying about everything and doing so with thanksgiving? Verse seven gives the answer:

Philippians 4:7 *And the peace of God, which passeth all understanding, shall keep your hearts and minds through Christ Jesus.*

Paul addressed people who had a lot to worry about. But when he told them not to worry, when he told them instead to pray over everything with thanksgiving, he said that the result would then be, not a solution to whatever the problem was, but the peace of God which passes all understanding keeping, guarding their hearts and minds through Christ Jesus.

Worry is not a substance; it is an emotion. As an emotion, it resides in the heart and mind, not the fingertips or feet. So when we make our default response to anything that troubles us an immediate retreat to the throne of God, a time of prayer and supplication, a time of thanksgiving for what God has already done, God will then garrison about our hearts and minds, He will set a guard around them, and fill us with peace that passes understanding.

There will be many times that you cannot understand; there will never be a time when there is not peace available that passes, that goes beyond understanding.

So, in seven short verses, Paul has taken us from people problems to peace. What point are you at in all of that?

Chapter Ten
Things

Philippians 4:8 *Finally, brethren, whatsoever things are true, whatsoever things are honest, whatsoever things are just, whatsoever things are pure, whatsoever things are lovely, whatsoever things are of good report; if there be any virtue, and if there be any praise, think on these things.* **9** *Those things, which ye have both learned, and received, and heard, and seen in me, do: and the God of peace shall be with you.*

In the last section of verses, Paul dealt with a prickly problem caused by feuding females. But he ended on a positive note, telling everyone how they could have the very precious gift of peace that passes all understanding. And now, in these two verses, he will deal with "things." I say that because he actually uses the word things eight times in just two verses!

Things to think

Philippians 4:8 *Finally, brethren, whatsoever things are true, whatsoever things are honest, whatsoever things are just, whatsoever things are pure, whatsoever things are lovely, whatsoever things are of good report; if there be any virtue, and if there be any praise, think on these things.*

A few chapters ago, I teased about Paul being a Baptist. All the way back at the beginning of chapter three, he was already using the word "finally," even though he was really nowhere near done. But now, as he again uses the word finally, he really is beginning to wrap things up. He once again addresses the believers in Philippi as brethren, the sixth of seven times[*] in the book that he will do so. And then he gives a lengthy sentence that would give a modern grammar teacher a headache. But it is written like it is written for a reason. Here is the sentence again:

...*Whatsoever things are true, whatsoever things are honest, whatsoever things are just, whatsoever things are pure, whatsoever things are lovely, whatsoever things are of good report; if there be any virtue, and if there be any praise, think on these things.*

An English grammar teacher today would be pretty quick to whip out a red pen on that sentence and change it along these lines:

Whatsoever things are true, honest, just, pure, lovely, and of good report, if there be any virtue and praise, think on them.

But in so doing, rigid modern grammar laws would rip much of the heart out of the passionate theology of this verse. You see, by using the "whatsoever things" descriptive in front of each and every item on the list, Paul is emphasizing each individual one. He is negating the idea that this is a buffet bar to be chosen from as our taste allows; he is commanding that we give equal attention and exceptional effort to every single one of them.

The command at the end of the verse is that we "think on these things." Think is from the word *logidzesthe,* and it means "to ponder, compute, reckon, and meditate." Albert Barnes put it this way, "Let them be the object of your careful attention and study, so as to practise them." (Linder)

---

[*]The eighth usage of the word, in Philippians 1:14, referred to brethren elsewhere.

114

So this is not just a fleeting thought crossing your mind at random times; this is an intentional focus of the mind that Paul is commanding. These things that he will list are things that we are to intentionally tune our minds toward and spend much time contemplating.

So, what exactly are we to be thinking about?

The first item on the list is things that are true. That is from the word *alaythay;* it is from the same word as that which I named my daughter, Alethia. In this case, it means true in the sense of "genuine, accurate, and real." We are to intentionally think on things that meet that criteria.

How often do we imagine offenses in our mind, even things that have never even remotely happened? How often do we hear something horrible or even too good to be true and simply believe it without question? How often do we speculate about people with no real foundation for the speculation? How often do we scroll the accounts of hateful online trolls who have salacious yet unverified things to say about preachers, churches, or just other believers?

All of this is antithetical to what is taught here. We are to intentionally settle our thinking into those things which are actually true, genuine, and real.

There are an infinite number of other areas to which this applies. Our minds always seem drawn to that which is sensational on the one hand or morbid on the other. And this makes us both gullible and also useful in the devil's hands. It makes us purveyors of harm rather than promoters of help.

We are to consistently think on those things that are true.

The second item on the list is things that are honest. And at first blush, you might be tempted to think this is merely a redundancy, a restatement of "true." But that is not the case. These items are related but not repetitive. Honest is from the word *semna,* and it means honest in the sense of "serious, of good character, honorable, respectable, and reputable." In other words, it is a focus on what is reputable versus what is disreputable.

If a girl tells you she wants to grow up to be a wife and mother, you smile with approval. If she tells you she wants to grow up to be a prostitute, you rightly throw a fit. One is an honest, reputable thing; the other is not.

If a boy tells you he wants to grow up to be a police officer or a soldier, you smile with approval. If he tells you he wants to grow up to be the leader of a drug cartel, you rightly throw a fit. One is an honest, reputable thing; the other is not.

If a girl tells you she wants to grow up to be a nurse or doctor, you smile with approval. If she tells you she wants to grow up to be a porn star, you rightly throw a fit. One is an honest, reputable thing; the other is not.

If a boy tells you he wants to grow up to be a pastor or missionary, you smile with approval. If he tells you he wants to grow up to be a communist, you rightly throw a fit. One is an honest, reputable thing; the other is not.

Everything in life will either be an honest, reputable thing or a dishonest, disreputable thing. Everything from TV shows to music to words themselves must be evaluated as such, and our thought life must respond to them appropriately.

We are to consistently think on those things that are honest.

The third item on the list is things that are just. That is from the word *dikaia*, and we get the word justified from it. It means "righteous, upright." It is an indication that something is morally acceptable to God.

Think of the limitless ways this can and should be applied! Our minds are to dwell on things that God Himself would not mind thinking about. They are to dwell on things that do not dirty our minds and hearts. Merely not doing wrong is not enough; we are to not think of wrong either.

Jesus Himself gave a fantastic example of this:

Matthew 5:27 *Ye have heard that it was said by them of old time, Thou shalt not commit adultery:* **28** *But I say unto you, That whosoever looketh on a woman to lust after her hath committed adultery with her already in his heart.*

Thinking wrong may not carry the immediate consequences of doing wrong, but thinking wrong is still doing wrong! It violates the command of Philippians 4:8 that we think on those things that are just, upright, morally pure.

The fourth item on the list is things that are pure. As with true and honest, you might be tempted to think this is merely a restatement of just, but it is not. Again, they are related but not repetitive. Pure is from the word *hagna,* which is from the same root word as the words holy and saint. It means "chaste and innocent."

We are to think on innocent things, not on dirty and salacious and questionable things. And social media has made that task much more difficult since dirty and salacious and questionable things make up such a huge amount of online fare.

Our humor is to be pure and innocent. Our reading choices are to be pure and innocent. Our interactions are to be pure and innocent.

We are to consistently think on those things that are pure.

The fifth item on the list is things that are lovely. That is from the word *prosphilay,* and it means "lovely in the sense of pleasant, agreeable, and amiable." Here is how Albert Barnes so eloquently put it:

> "A Christian should not be sour, crabbed, and irritable in his temper, for nothing almost tends so much to injure the cause of religion as a temper always chafed; a brow morose and stern; an eye that is severe and unkind, and a disposition to find fault with everything." (Linder)

In other words, we are to refrain from always finding the negative to complain about, and we are to intentionally find the positive to be grateful for.

A good many years ago, a couple joined our church. After several weeks, I noticed a rather odd thing. Our ladies, who were always so friendly to everyone, were acting strangely stand-offish to this woman. I mean, to such a degree that the woman had developed her own personal bubble. No matter where she sat in church, there would be no one within six feet of her! The place could be packed, and yet she would still have her bubble. It stuck out like a sore thumb!

I finally started asking some questions. As it turns out, this lady, who, of all things, was married to a man who was training for the ministry, was the most negatively focused woman on earth. No matter what anyone said, at all, ever, she had something negative to say about it.

Dana pulled her aside and talked to her repeatedly, to no avail whatsoever.

So I decided to fix the problem before she took it into the ministry with her and ruined both her husband and everyone they ministered to.

On a Sunday morning, I stood in the pulpit before church, just writing a few things down, waiting...

The woman and her husband walked in, and it took about ten seconds for her to say something negative. I immediately and loudly said, "That's one!" Everyone just sort of stared at me. I ignored them and kept on scribbling.

Less than a minute later, she said something else snarky and negative. I loudly said, "That's two!" Once again, everyone just sort of stared at me. I ignored them and kept on scribbling, but I knew that by then, my people were catching on to what this was all about.

Less than a minute later, a third negative comment, followed by me once again nearly shouting, "That's three!"

When I did, the woman said, "Preacher, what are you doing?" I smiled sweetly and said, "I'm going to count out loud every single negative comment you make today."

Harsh? Paul probably wouldn't have thought so since, just a few verses earlier, he called Euodias and Syntyche out by name for their catfighting. And since she had already repeatedly brushed aside private attempts to correct the issue, I really did not know of any better way to handle it!

Our thoughts are not to dwell on the negative. They are to dwell on things that are lovely, things that are pleasant, agreeable, and amiable.

We are to consistently think on those things that are lovely.

The sixth item on the list is things that are of good report. Good report is from the word *euphayma*, and it means "commendable."

This is clearly a pretty broad term. Any good behavior fits under this heading. Children obeying their parents, wives honoring their husbands, husbands loving their wives as Christ loves the church, tipping well in restaurants, not airing dirty laundry online, things that are of good report.

If anything we think about would embarrass us if it were turned into a video and shown to the world, we shouldn't be thinking about it. If anything we think about would make God smile, we should be thinking about it.

We are to consistently think on those things that are of good report.

After listing these six items, Paul changes the grammar just a bit and says, "*if there be any virtue, and if there be any praise, think on these things.*" What he is doing in these words is acknowledging that he could never produce an exhaustive list of things we ought to be thinking about, so he, at this point, wants to give two general guidelines for anything further to think about

His first guideline is that if something has any virtue to it, we should be thinking about it. Virtue is from the word *aretay,* and it means "excellence, especially in a moral sense." Adam Clarke said of this, "If they be calculated to promote the general good of mankind." (507)

Think of how broad that can be! It includes everything from truly good and wholesome artwork, good and clean entertainment, training in good manners, a good work ethic, edifying music, the applications are near limitless. If something is excellent in the sense of beneficial to man without being displeasing to God, it fits this criterion.

We are to consistently think on those things that are of virtue.

His second guideline is that if there be any praise to something, we should be thinking about it. This phrase means if there is something truly worthy of being praised, we should be thinking about it.

Staying a virgin until marriage is worthy of being praised. Being faithful to your spouse is worthy of being praised. Being faithful to church is worthy of being praised. Finding a cure for cancer is worthy of being praised. Working hard is worthy of being praised. Handling money well is worthy of being praised. Standing up for the innocent is worthy of being praised. Winning souls is worthy of being praised. Again, the applications are near limitless.

If something is truly worthy of praise, it fits this criterion. We are to consistently think on those things that are praiseworthy.

This is not a small matter, first of all because actions spring from thoughts, but also because even our thoughts themselves are utterly known to God:

Hebrews 4:12 *For the word of God is quick, and powerful, and sharper than any twoedged sword, piercing even to the dividing asunder of soul and spirit, and of the joints and* *marrow, <u>and is a discerner of the thoughts and intents of the</u> <u>heart</u>. 13 Neither is there any creature that is not manifest in his sight: but all things are naked and opened unto the eyes of him with whom we have to do.*

Do not ever excuse your bad thoughts; expunge and exchange your bad thoughts.

Things to do

Philippians 4:9 *Those **things**, which ye have both learned, and received, and heard, and seen in me, do: and the God of peace shall be with you.*

Paul is still writing about things. But now, he switches from things to think about to things to do. And it is interesting the multi-faceted way that he mentions this. He says, *"Those things, which ye have both **learned**, and **received**, and **heard**, and **seen** in me, do..."*

There are two complementary pairs in these four words.

Paul first of all reminded the brethren in Philippi that they had learned and received some things from him. This means that he had preached and taught and written to them, and they had taken it all in. This was a matter of him being a teacher and them being students.

His second reminder was that they had heard and seen some things in him. This was a matter of him being the living example and them being the followers of that example.

So, after telling them at length how to think, he much more briefly told them how to behave. And his words were simple: *If I taught it to you, do it, and if you saw it or heard it in me, do it.*

Think about that. Paul was actually able to put that in writing for that and all future generations to see! Could we do the same? If not, there is a problem with us that needs to be addressed. We are all supposed to be both accurate teachers of the Word and accurate followers of the Word of God. People legitimately ought to be able to follow both our words and our walk.

But another facet of this is that we ourselves are to follow Paul's words and Paul's example. He is the right model of what a follower of Christ ought to be. He was passionate for souls, passionate about mission work, passionate about the written Word of God (both Old and New Testaments) and a godly man. No, he was not perfect; we can see that from the fallout with Barnabas. But you will be hard-pressed to find a better overall model of a true disciple of Christ.

After telling them what to do, he closed with the words *"and the God of peace shall be with you."* And this is exactly what it appears to be, an effect from a cause. When we do right, God will be with us in a peace-giving manner. When we do wrong, He will not be with us in a peace-giving manner; He will be with us in a chastening manner.

———————————————

This is all about things, things to think about and things to do. If we think about the right things and if we do the right things, we get the right results.

Chapter Eleven
Precious Promises

Philippians 4:10 *But I rejoiced in the Lord greatly, that now at the last your care of me hath flourished again; wherein ye were also careful, but ye lacked opportunity.* **11** *Not that I speak in respect of want: for I have learned, in whatsoever state I am, therewith to be content.* **12** *I know both how to be abased, and I know how to abound: every where and in all things I am instructed both to be full and to be hungry, both to abound and to suffer need.* **13** *I can do all things through Christ which strengtheneth me.* **14** *Notwithstanding ye have well done, that ye did communicate with my affliction.* **15** *Now ye Philippians know also, that in the beginning of the gospel, when I departed from Macedonia, no church communicated with me as concerning giving and receiving, but ye only.* **16** *For even in Thessalonica ye sent once and again unto my necessity.* **17** *Not because I desire a gift: but I desire fruit that may abound to your account.* **18** *But I have all, and abound: I am full, having received of Epaphroditus the things which were sent from you, an odour of a sweet smell, a sacrifice acceptable, wellpleasing to God.* **19** *But my God shall supply all your need according to his riches in glory by Christ Jesus.*

We covered just two verses in the last chapter, but those verses gave us a very long list of things to think and to do. The verses that we will now cover, though, are both more lengthy and more famous. In fact, two of them are famous to the point of being some of the most misused verses in the Bible, mostly due to them constantly being yanked out of their context. And that is a shame because, properly understood, they are some of the most precious promises in the Bible.

Care for God's man

Philippians 4:10 *But I rejoiced in the Lord greatly, that now at the last your care of me hath flourished again; wherein ye were also careful, but ye lacked opportunity.*

For a time, the Philippian church had supported Paul in his missionary and ministerial endeavors; they had made sure that he had the funds to live on and to work with. But when Paul got to Rome, the distance between the two made that very difficult. The Philippians still wanted to help; they were careful, meaning of the mind to do so, as Paul observed. But though they had the desire, they lacked the opportunity.

And then came the chance to send Epaphroditus to Rome and have him bring another offering to Paul. When Epaphroditus showed up with those funds, Paul *rejoiced in the Lord greatly.*

Paul was not some pampered prosperity pimp preacher; he was a genuine man of God who worked like a dog in the ministry and who, on occasion, even did secular work (tent-making) to support himself while in the ministry. He was truly worthy of what the church at Philippi gave him and doubtless worthy of much more besides.

From time to time, you will come across people who believe that preachers should not get a paycheck. People like that believe the opposite of Paul and are not to be taken seriously. They themselves would never work for free and are being hypocritical by expecting preachers to do so.

Contentment in everything

Philippians 4:11 *Not that I speak in respect of want: for I have learned, in whatsoever state I am, therewith to be content.* **12** *I know both how to be abased, and I know how to abound: every where and in all things I am instructed both to be full and to be hungry, both to abound and to suffer need.*

Paul is still continuing on the same line of thought; he will do so all the way through verse nineteen. Having told the Philippians in verse ten how much he appreciated the financial help they sent him, he quickly moves into the thought of verse eleven. And that thought is that he is not speaking out of want, meaning out of lack. God had always met his needs and would always do so!

After telling them that he was not speaking from want, he said, *"for I have learned, in whatsoever state I am, therewith to be content."* And he will not take long at all to elaborate on that: his very next words were, *"I know both how to be abased, and I know how to abound: every where and in all things I am instructed both to be full and to be hungry, both to abound and to suffer need."*

So, Paul was indicating that he had learned how to be content when he had more money than he knew what to do with and when he was too poor to even buy groceries. None of us would likely have any trouble with the former condition, but a whole lot would likely have trouble with the latter!

It is interesting that Paul said he was *instructed* both to be full and to be hungry, to abound and to suffer need. God literally taught him both to be okay with prosperity and with poverty!

In the early days of Dana and I starting Cornerstone, we were instructed on poverty. Right after the church took us on full-time and I gave up my jewelry store to be full-time, the offerings absolutely tanked. We went six weeks without a paycheck and never said a word. And God met every single one of our needs! A few years later, the church was in a bit of a better position, and we started having kids, so they decided to buy us a vehicle to carry them in. It was a ten-year-old Yukon with pretty high miles for just a few thousand dollars. And that is when I was surprised by a man who threw a little bit of a fit because he was quite certain he could have gotten something cheaper at govdeals.com!

Because nothing says "I love you" like a thirty year old Rambler.

But now, as of the writing of this book, we are twenty-six years in, and we are actually doing okay financially and the church just bought Dana a new vehicle, the first one she has ever owned. We do not feel worthy, but we do enjoy it! We have been instructed to be okay with "prosperity" just as much as we were instructed to be okay with poverty!

Please understand something at this point. This principle does not just apply to preachers; it applies to all believers. Every last one of us is to take whatever God gives us or whatever He withholds from us with gratefulness and, here is the word Paul used, contentment.

There is such a lack of contentment among believers. And I mean, even among believers whose needs are all very well supplied! It is almost like we have forgotten that this world is not our home; we are just strangers and pilgrims passing through.

Now, get all of that in your mind. Everything that Paul has just said is the context for what comes next; one of the two verses I spoke of earlier that far too often gets taken completely out of context. Here is that verse:

Philippians 4:13 *I can do all things through Christ which strengtheneth me.*

Behold, the touchdown scoring, three point shooting, home run hitting verse of Scripture. This verse gets slapped on everything from sports to academic achievements to political races. But it has a context, and the context has nothing to do with any of those things. The context has to do with being able to handle poverty or prosperity with contentment. The context has to do with being happy sleeping on a feather bed or on a dungeon floor. The context has to do with being free or being in chains. The context has to do with being too full to eat another bite or so hungry that you are quite certain you are going to starve to death.

You can do all things through Christ who strengthens you. You can be content through the times when your bills are past due and the roof is leaking and the car is being repossessed and you just got laid off. You may not *like* those times, but you can be *content* through those times because you can do all things through Christ who strengthens you.

Simply put, the contentment of a believer does not come from the outside in; it comes from the inside out. We are not content because pleasant things are all around us; we are content because the Christ who strengthens us is within us.

Communication from the wallet

Philippians 4:14 *Notwithstanding ye have well done, that ye did communicate with my affliction.*

Paul just got done telling the Philippians that he could be just as content in poverty as he was in prosperity. But he immediately went to "*notwithstanding*" to start verse fourteen. That word basically means nevertheless. Paul told them here in verse fourteen that even though he could be content in poverty, they nevertheless did well by communicating with his affliction. And the very next verse leaves no doubt whatsoever what he meant by that:

Philippians 4:15 *Now ye Philippians know also, that in the beginning of the gospel, when I departed from Macedonia,* *no church communicated with me as concerning giving and receiving, but ye only.*

He was talking about them supporting him financially. They had *"well done"* when they did so. And here, in verse fifteen, we learn that at the time he left Macedonia, they were the only church that did so!

Paul had come to Macedonia after receiving the vision of a man from Macedonia saying, *"Come over into Macedonia, and help us,"* in **Acts 16:9**. So he went. And while he was there, he was beaten horribly in Philippi. Then he was forced out of Thessalonica. Then he was forced out of Berea. Paul really went through hell itself to get the gospel to people in that area of the world! And yet, when he left, only one single church supported him financially: only the church at Philippi.

Philippians 4:16 *For even in Thessalonica ye sent once and again unto my necessity.* **17** *Not because I desire a gift: but I desire fruit that may abound to your account.*

These verses show that the church at Philippi started supporting Paul early on. Even when he was still just in Thessalonica, only a hundred miles or so away, they multiple times sent money to meet his needs. But as Paul was writing this, he seems very much to have anticipated the snarky spirit of the critic, the person who would, in any age, slap the age-old insult on a preacher, "He's just in it for the money." That I find to be the most ironic accusation on earth; there are a tiny handful of charlatan, prosperity-pimp preachers in our land and about a million other preachers who could make way more doing something else, but who continue to minister because it is a calling, not a career.

So, heading the critic off at the pass, Paul pointed out in verse seventeen that he was not desirous of a gift, and that simply means that he was not in it for the money nor interested in their money for his own sake. Instead, he was desirous for fruit to abound to their account. Do you realize what that means? It means that by investing in Paul's ministry, they were recipients with him of the credit and of the blessings of every soul that was won and every church that was begun! You see, not everyone can go by going – but everyone can go by giving. When you support a missionary or a pastor, the work that they do goes on your account as well as theirs.

Is it a good investment? Well, in Paul's case, it certainly was. I would call it the ecclesiological equivalent of buying stock in Apple the day it was offered in 1980 at $10 a share on a split-adjusted basis and now seeing it at $194 a share today. Paul likely won more souls to Christ than any other living human, and the Philippians shared the credit for all of them since their giving made it possible. At the Judgment Seat of Christ, they will be rewarded right alongside him for everything done in his ministry through their giving!

Confidence in God's supply

Philippians 4:18 *But I have all, and abound: I am full, having received of Epaphroditus the things which were sent from you, an odour of a sweet smell, a sacrifice acceptable, wellpleasing to God.*

Paul gets very personal and very up-to-the-moment in this verse. He was sitting there with the gift they sent by the hand of Epaphroditus. And he wanted them to know that it was more than enough. He said, *"I have all, and abound: I am full."* That was an eloquent way of saying, "I don't need any more; I have more than enough."

This once again shows the pure character of Paul. The man was not a money-grubber, or in Biblical terms, he was not greedy of filthy lucre. When he had enough, he said so.

Look at the last part of verse eighteen to see how he described what they sent from God's point of view:

...an odour of a sweet smell, a sacrifice acceptable, wellpleasing to God.

The odor of a sweet smell harkened back to the incense that was often offered to God. Do you know why human beings love to smell sweet things? Because we are made in the image of God, and He loves to smell sweet things. And what the Philippians sent to Paul smelled very sweet to God.

The sacrifice, acceptable, well pleasing to God, takes us back in time as far as Genesis 4 and the radically different sacrifices of Cain and Abel. God was well pleased by the type and quality of sacrifice that Abel brought but very displeased by the type and quality of sacrifice that Cain brought. God wants and deserves our best. When He looked at what the Philippians sent Paul, He regarded it as the best, just like what Abel brought thousands of years before.

And now let me repeat what I said just before we covered verse thirteen. Get all of what we have just covered in your mind. Everything that Paul has just said is the context for what comes next; the other of the two verses I spoke of earlier that far too often gets taken completely out of context. Here is that verse:

Philippians 4:19 *But my God shall supply all your need according to his riches in glory by Christ Jesus.*

That verse gets quoted and sung and printed and posted all the time. But just like verse thirteen, it has a context. And the context is in giving to missions and ministry! When we stretch out to support missions and ministry, we can confidently expect that God will supply all of our actual needs, not barely, but abundantly, according to his riches in glory by Christ Jesus. He does not supply based on our worth here on earth but on His own wealth in glory!

These are not idle words to me. I have not just tithed consistently in my life; I also started giving to missions when I was sixteen years old, and I mean giving generously. And I can tell you after all of these years that I have not missed a single meal for lack of money and that God has taken very good care

130

of me. I have found the promise of Philippians 4:19 to be abundantly, personally true in my life.

Was Paul a preacher who always talked about money? Certainly not. But did he shy away from the subject when it was warranted? Again, certainly not. And we should be very glad of it. These ten verses give some of the clearest guidance in the Bible about money and ministry, and without them, many ministers and ministries through the ages would doubtless have struggled greatly.

Chapter Twelve
A Joyful Farewell

Philippians 4:20 *Now unto God and our Father be glory for ever and ever. Amen.* **21** *Salute every saint in Christ Jesus. The brethren which are with me greet you.* **22** *All the saints salute you, chiefly they that are of Caesar's household.*

Philippians has been a joyful book, and the last section of verses certainly was. They contained some of the most precious promises in the Bible, promises regarding being able to do all things through Christ, and of God providing for our needs, promises that, when taken in context, should be some of the main "go-to passages" for believers.

These last few verses will simply be Paul's joyful farewell to this happy letter that was mostly a thank-you note for their mission support.

A call to glory

Philippians 4:20 *Now unto God and our Father be glory for ever and ever. Amen.*

In this instance, the words God and Father are referring to one person, not two, God the Father, the first member of the Trinity. Think of *and* here as an intertwining word rather than an individualizing word. For instance, if I spoke of my wife and best friend, I would be speaking of one person, not two, since my wife is my best friend.

As Paul began to bring this joyful epistle to the church at Philippi to a close, he could not seem to refrain from a torrent of happy emotions directed toward the One who made all of his happiness possible, God the Father. When he said, "*Now unto God and our Father be glory for ever and ever,*" he was expressing his personal wish and his heartfelt evaluation of what God deserved.

Paul wanted God to receive glory. And He wanted Him to receive glory, not just for a little while, but forever and ever. The phrase those words come from is *tous aionos tone aionone.* If a couple of those words sound like our word for eons, it is because our word eons does, in fact, come from that doubled Greek word.

Eons are immeasurably long periods of time; ages, as they are often called. So this forever and ever that Paul wanted God to be glorified in was not just in our age, our human, earthly, "forever," it was literally forever and ever, throughout all the ages, going beyond time, beyond the destruction of this heaven and earth and universe, on into the new heaven and new earth, and never ceasing throughout all of that eternity.

And to add a theological exclamation point on that desire, Paul said, "*Amen!*"

You should try that sometime; you just might like it!

A cheerful salute

Philippians 4:21 *Salute every saint in Christ Jesus. The brethren which are with me greet you.* **22a** *All the saints salute you...*

If there is one thing that the lost world knows (and usually despises) about the Bible, it is that it is loaded with commands, things like, "Thou shalt not steal; thou shalt not kill; thou shalt not commit adultery."

But in reality, it is even worse or better than they know, depending upon your perspective. You see, the Bible has more commands than most people realize, and some of them are absolutely joyous commands! What you see in the first words of verse twenty-one is one of those commands. When Paul said, *"Salute every saint in Christ Jesus,"* in grammatical terms, he wrote it as an imperative command. To salute does not mean to raise your hand to your hat as our military personnel do; it simply means to greet, to bid welcome, to receive joyfully. And you should know that the word greet, that we will come to just one phrase later, is from the exact same word as the words for salute in verses twenty-one and twenty-two. He uses that word three times in short order, and the change from salute to greet in the second usage is merely for variety since either one is an absolutely accurate translation of *aspadzomia*.

So again, concerning the saints, other believers, Paul's command is that we greet them, bid them welcome, and receive them joyfully. And if you are sitting there reading this and thinking, "Well, that doesn't sound so hard," then you have probably either not been saved for very long or have not paid attention to the church world. I do not mean in the least to be a Debbie downer, but Christians can often be far more cordial to lost reprobates than they are to one another. It will not take you long, especially online, to see Christians being as sweet as sugar to politicians and sports stars and singers and absolutely savage one to another.

That is not what we should be known for. Yes, we are going to disagree on things from time to time, and yes, there is even a command to exercise church discipline when needed under some very specific circumstances, and there are also repeated commands that we call out heresy and contend for the faith. But bluntly, far, far too often, what we see is just Christians being jerks to each other rather than being cordial to each other.

It is almost like we have forgotten that we are going to be living together forever.

A pretty long while back, another preacher got in a meeting with other preachers, a meeting that I was the subject of. And along with all of the rest of them, he raised his hand to blackball me from their number.

Fast forward probably fifteen years. The man had a heart attack and ended up in a hospital not too far from me. So I got in the car and went to see him; we had not seen each other in all of those long years. When I walked in, his eyes got huge; I think maybe he thought I was going to cut off his oxygen! But that was not what I was there for. I was there because I was the nearest preacher to where he was in that hospital, so I was the natural choice for a fellow pastor to go and pray for him in person.

He and I are not likely to ever have a cookout together, and we certainly are not going to take any joint selfies. But I am saved, and he is saved, and that makes us family, and I want to do my best to behave as such. You see, Paul did not command that we salute every one of our tiny circle of saints; he commanded that we salute every saint.

Paul closed out verse twenty-one with the words, *"The brethren which are with me greet you."*

There is a pretty happy thing to notice in those words: Paul was not alone. In his hour of imprisonment, in his hour of uncertainty, there were people there with him, and those people wanted to send greetings along with him to the believers in Philippi.

One of the best things you can ever do for your brothers and sisters in Christ is to simply be with them. Be in church with them. Be in the waiting room of the hospital with them. Be at the altar with them. Be there to cry with them when they are crying. Be there to rejoice with them when they are rejoicing. A person who does not want to be around other Christians may possibly be saved, but they are certainly not behaving as a Christian. The Christ that we get the word Christian from wanted to be with His men.

Paul then began verse twenty-two with another word of salutation, *"All the saints salute you."* One phrase earlier, Paul had spoken of the brethren that were with him. And now he expands the circle and speaks of all believers in that area that he has gotten to know. All of them communicated to him to please tell the Philippians hello for them when he wrote to them. There was such a camaraderie in the early church; we would do well to cultivate that in our churches today!

A chief reminder

Philippians 4:22 *All the saints salute you, <u>chiefly they that are of Caesar's household</u>.*

Let me remind you of what I said way back when we covered Philippians 1:13, where Paul spoke of people in the palace getting saved, which is exactly what he is again referencing as he draws this letter to a close. People in Caesar's household heard the gospel from Paul and got saved! And when you know who that "Caesar" was, it makes it all the more remarkable. Notice what Adam Clarke said of this:

"Nero was at this time emperor of Rome: a more worthless, cruel, and diabolic wretch never disgraced the name or form of man; yet in his family there were Christians." (508)

We will meet and speak to people in Nero's family in heaven because of what Paul went through. Let that sink in! Can you imagine any other circumstance under which they would ever even hear of the gospel? Do you imagine for even a moment that Paul would have been able simply to travel to Rome, knock on the door of the palace, and say, "Hi, I'm Paul. I'm from the church down the road, and I just wanted to talk to you for a few moments about Jesus..."

The only way in the world he would ever get inside the palace with the gospel is to be brought there in chains.

But for the Philippians, as they read the next to closing words of this letter, what it meant was that their investment had been worth it. They supported a good man of God, a missionary in this case, and that investment paid off. Some of the least likely people on earth to ever get saved got saved. And they go so very saved that, when Paul wrote a letter back to the church at Philippi, they made sure to tell him to greet that church for them!

Your investment in the work of God does make a difference.

A closing note

Philippians 4:23 *The grace of our Lord Jesus Christ be with you all. Amen. <To the Philippians written from Rome, by Epaphroditus.>*

Paul closed this joyful letter with a wish that the grace, in this case, the grace for everyday living, would be with his precious brethren in Philippi. Whether he lived or not was still an open question; how he felt about them was definitely not. And then Paul added the note that this epistle had been transcribed and carried back to them by their very own Epaphroditus.

And you surely know that when he walked in the door of their church with that letter in his hand, the treasures of joy became even more precious to them.

Works Cited

Lindner, P. (2003). Power Bible CD Version (5.9). *Power Bible.*, https://powerbible.com/. 2010/09/14.

Clarke, A. (1977). *The Holy Bible, containing the Old and New Testaments, the text carefully printed from the most correct copies of the present authorized translation, including the marginal readings and parallel texts: With a commentary and critical notes designed as a help to a better understanding of the sacred writings* (Vol. 6). Abingdon Press.

Jamieson, R., Fausset, A. R., & Brown, D. (2008). *A commentary on the Old and New Testaments* (Vol. 3). Hendrickson Publishers.

Qurollo, J. A. (2007). *Notes on Philippians*. Qurollo Publishing.

Other Books by Dr. Wagner

Daniel: Breathtaking
Ephesians: The Treasures of Family
Esther: Five Feasts and the Fingerprints of God
Galatians: The Treasures of Liberty
James: The Pen and the Plumb Line
Jonah: A Story of Greatness
Nehemiah: A Labor of Love
Proverbs Vol 1: Bright Light from Dark Sayings
Proverbs Vol 2: Bright Light from Dark Sayings
The Revelation: Ready or Not
Romans: Salvation from A-Z
Ruth: Diamonds in the Darkness
Beyond the Colored Coat
From Footers to Finish Nails
Learning Not to Fear the Old Testament
Marriage Makers/Marriage Breakers
I'm Saved! Now What???
Don't Muzzle the Ox

Devotionals

DO Drops Vol. 1
DO Drops Vol. 2
DO Drops Vol. 3
DO Drops Vol. 4
DO Drops Vol. 5
DO Drops Vol. 6
DO Drops Vol. 7
DO Drops Vol. 8
DO Drops Vol. 9
DO Drops Vol 10
DO Drops Vol 11

Books in the Night Heroes Series

Cry from the Coal Mine (Vol 1)
Free Fall (Vol 2)
Broken Brotherhood (Vol 3)
The Blade of Black Crow (Vol 4)
Ghost Ship (Vol 5)
When Serpents Rise (Vol 6)
Moth Man (Vol 7)
Runaway (Vol 8)
Terror by Day (Vol 9)
Winter Wolf (Vol 10)
Desert Heat (Vol 11)
Deadline (Vol 12)

Other Fiction

Zak Blue: Falcon Wing
Zak Blue: Enter the Maelstrom

www.ingramcontent.com/pod-product-compliance
Lightning Source LLC
Chambersburg PA
CBHW072022040426

42447CB00009B/1692